COOKING FOR THE LOVE OF THE WORLD

COOKING FOR THE LOVE OF THE WORLD

Awakening Our Spirituality through Cooking

ANNE-MARIE FRYER WIBOLTT

with pencil illustrations by the Author

Foreword by Robert Sardello

GOLDENSTONE PRESS *Benson, North Carolina*

HEAVEN & EARTH PUBLISHING *East Montpelier, Vermont*

Published by Goldenstone Press and Heaven & Earth Publishing

ISBN: 978-0-9779825-5-4

Cover art and page 45 art, copyright © 2008 by Leo Klein

Book design by Richard Wehrman
www.merlinwood.net

10 9 8 7 6 5 4 3 2 1

GOLDENSTONE PRESS

GOLDENSTONE PRESS seeks to make original spiritual thought available as a force of individual, cultural and world revitalization. The press is an integral dimension of the work of the School of Spiritual Psychology. The mission of the School includes restoring the book as a way of inner transformation and awakening to spirit. We recognize that secondary thought and the reduction of books to sources of information and entertainment as the dominant meaning of reading places in jeopardy the unique character of writing as a vessel of the human spirit. We feel that the continuing emphasis of such a narrowing of what books are intended to be needs to be balanced by writing, editing and publishing that emphasizes the act of reading as entering into a magical, even miraculous spiritual realm that stimulates the imagination and makes possible discerning reality from illusion in the world. The editorial board of Goldenstone Press is committed to fostering authors with the capacity of creative spiritual imagination who write in forms that bring readers into deep engagement with an inner transformative process rather than being spectators to someone's speculations. A complete catalogue of all our books may be found at www.goldenstonepress.com.

TO THE SPIRIT OF LOVE

TABLE OF CONTENTS

FOREWORD BY ROBERT SARDELLO   xi

MY JOURNEY   xvi

INTRODUCTION   1

RHYTHMS IN THE WORLD   5

     The Yearly Seasonal Cycles   6
     The Rhythms of the Day   7

A WISDOM-FILLED WORLD   9

     Creative Life Forces   10
     Nature Beings in the World   13
     The Living World Today   15

THE CYCLE AND RHYTHMS OF A PLANT   16

     Grounding Roots   17
     Magic between Root and Stem   18
     Light Leafy Greens   19
     Intensification between Stem and Flower   20
     Magnificent Flower   20
     Heavy Sweetness of Fruits   21
     Sun-Ripened Seeds   21
     Golden Grains   22
     Living into the Flowing Activity of Life   23

COLLECTING VEGETABLES   25

THE WATER OF LIFE   28

     Messages from Water   29
     Cooking Water   30
     Treasures from the Pulsing Sea   31

CELEBRATING THE SEASONAL FESTIVALS   33
   Cooking, an Essential Aspect of a Spiritual Path   35
   A Gift for Nature   35

A LIVING RELATIONSHIP WITH THE LAND   37

COOKING AS A LIVING ART   39
   Entering the Kitchen   41
   Attending to Attentiveness   42

COOKING WITH NATURE   45
   Cutting Styles—The Harmony of Form   47
   Cooking Styles   50
   Seasonal Cooking Styles   51
   Natural Flavors of Life   56
   Flexibility in Following Recipes   57

CREATING BALANCED MEALS   60
   Soups   61
   Whole Grains and Breads   62
   Seasonal Vegetables and Fruits   63
   Animal Foods, Dairy, and Beans   64
   Oils, Fats, Seeds, and Nuts   65
   Seasonings   65
   Cultured and Fermented Foods   66
   Desserts   67
   The Finishing Touch   67

AT THE TABLE   69
   Grace   69
   Savoring the Food   70
   Digestion, a Celebration of Life   71

RECIPE SECTION

STARTING NEW—COOKING FOR SPRING   73

    Early Spring Menu   75
    Celebration of Spring Menu   82
    Late Spring Menu   95

BLOSSOMING AND MATURING—COOKING FOR SUMMER   101

    Early Summer Menu   104
    Celebration of Summer Menu   113
    Late Summer Menu   125

DRAWING IN—COOKING FOR AUTUMN   131

    Early Autumn Menu   134
    Celebration of Autumn Menu   142
    Late Autumn Menu   153

NOURISHING THE INNER LIGHT—COOKING FOR WINTER   161

    Early Winter Menu   163
    Celebration of Winter Menu   170
    Late Winter Menu   181

RECIPE INDEX   187

BIBLIOGRAPHY   191

RESOURCES   196

NATURAL HEALTH COUNSELING FOR LIFE   201

FOREWORD

This highly unusual and oh, so significant writing takes something we all do every day, several times—eating—and helps infuse this act with a deeply reverent and spiritual consciousness. The book accomplishes this intention by brilliantly and beautifully placing food within an understanding of the earthly and cosmic forces of plant life as well as providing exquisite recipes that transform nature into the art of cooking.

It might be helpful to forewarn you just a bit by urging you to work with the whole of the book. Because of our tendency to compartmentalize our actions, there may be a temptation to look upon this book as two books rather than one—a book on the spirituality of food and a practical cookbook. But Anne-Marie is very clear in what she is doing with this writing. She helps us perceive our bodies, our lives, the world around us, and the larger universe as a whole form of multiple, related activities that come together in miraculous ways through the act of eating. Until we can consciously enter into the miracle of food, we are lost in one popular speculation after another concerning how to eat.

Miraculous is a good word, one I want to introduce as describing the experience you enter as you read this book. The wealth of information that is now available concerning nutrition, calories, carbohydrates, and the thousands of diets available to help us achieve some notion of health and ideal figure, goes beyond anyone's capacity to comprehend. What has been lacking until now is an entirely new way of understanding food and eating. And gosh, no, not another theory that takes on the status of a trend that will change in a year or two!

This writing is far more radical than that. It invites us into the joy of paying attention to the magnificent beauty of nature, not as some brief ecstatic moment of experience, but carefully, lovingly, and continually. As we do so, over time, we develop an entirely new relation to food because we have overcome the spectator perspective and become engaged with being intimately interwoven with the world and, indeed, with the cosmos.

By far the most significant aspect of paying this kind of new attention to the natural world in relation to food and eating is to begin, slowly, to live into the element of rhythm that characterizes the movements of the cosmos, the earth, and the human body. The rhythms of the days, the seasons, the years, of morning, noon, evening, of waking and sleeping, and of expansion and contraction, intertwine with the rhythms of plant life. These natural rhythms and their relationships one to another are severely disrupted, so it is hardly surprising that pathologies of eating are rampant, ranging from the obvious epidemic of obesity to the more secret epidemics of anorexia and bulimia. Neither psychological answers nor fewer carbs nor fast-food lettuce and tomatoes rather than fast-food hamburgers are likely to do much, because all of these ways of trying to address eating pathologies neglect the necessary element of *rhythm*. More than anything else, this book is about refinding our place in the great natural motions of the cosmos as manifested in the growth of the foods we eat. Eating can be a way of coming home to our place within the cosmos.

The kind of language I am using to open the door to your reading is quite different than the mode of speaking you will find within these pages. Anne-Marie is a gifted writer because she is a gifted observer. There is a term for this kind of engaged, loving, participant observation. It is called *phenomenology*. The intent of this kind of observing is to allow the phenomenon to reveal itself rather than imposing our constructs and theories in order to understand. This book is full of this kind of observing, and as you read, you will find yourself taken back into the world as it appeared when you were a child—except then you perhaps did not have the words to describe the wonders and mysteries of the unfolding of the plant world.

There is a kind of second innocence to this writing, and for that reason you can trust it without reservation. There is no attempt to convince you of the merits of this way of looking at the world, at food, and at eating. The phenomenon itself convinces, once you can see.

This holistic approach to food is why you must read the book as a whole. If you simply go to the recipes and try them, it is likely that you will soon move on to others in other places. If, however, you study the writing, you will feel the wonders of the world, and the recipes will be flavored by the devoted attention that you now give to the world.

You are about to be refreshingly astounded by a writing on food that concentrates on qualities rather than quantities. There is no mention anywhere in this book about how many calories you should take in or how many carbohydrates. The living world is a world of exquisite and particular qualities. The world of the dead is the world of quantities. Thus, we cannot be nourished by theories of eating that are founded on the imagination of dead things. When we do embrace such views about food and find some results for a while, we are equally astounded to find that the pounds eventually come back. Materialistic approaches to nutrition, food, and dieting can only yield concern for quantities, to the point of obsession. These approaches to food are part of the problem of commodification that they try to address and cannot solve, because the theories of these approaches, which concentrate on food as commodity, exist at the same level as the problem.

When we think of spirituality or "being spiritual," we tend to think of how to be less of this world and more part of a nonmaterial realm. That kind of spirituality does not characterize this book. And, it is true, when you do find nutritional interests among spiritually oriented folk, there is something that tends to be just a little bit wispy about those interests. Often the notion is that it is necessary to purify the body in order to be spiritual. Or it is necessary to refrain from eating meat and meat products in order to be fully spiritual.

The notion of the spiritual realms that you will find in this writing is much more embracing of the world. While the pollution and contamination of foods is certainly something that this book tries to get us to move away from, that has to do with the way in which food has been deadened before it gets to the table, deadened by chemical fertilizers, genetically engineered seeds, and chemical preservatives. But the fullness of the world and all that is offered by nature as gift is embraced. What we are given here is food and eating as everyday festival.

A very important transition is made in this writing as Anne-Marie moves carefully from descriptions of plants and the natural world to the art of cooking. The core of this art is to consciously work with the rhythms of the natural world, to intensify them into smell, touch, and taste in such a manner that we are taken even further into being a part of world-rhythm. There is a radical secret here—namely, that if we cook and eat reverently, not with false piety, but genuinely experiencing the cosmic processes of expansion and contraction in the preparation of food, then we are serving the world in our eating. Imagine that! Eating can be renewing for the earth, not just for ourselves! It makes perfect sense. If we are bodily deadened by what and how we eat, then we will perceive the world as mere objects to be used to keep the engine running. If, on the other hand, we see the world in its living activity, feel the connection of this life to the life of the body, and prepare food and eat in relation to these living qualities, we will perceive the earth as a living being: embodied ecology.

While I may seem to pit the artistic qualities of this book against the harsh, quantitative approach of scientific nutrition, I do not intend to oppose art and science. In fact, the kind of observations that fill this book, in many ways, satisfy the most basic aspect of science: to observe carefully and clearly without prejudice. The observations of the plant world described herein satisfy this basic tenet of science.

While this writing is without question also artistic, it might be helpful to clarify how I am using the term *artistic*. I use it in two senses with respect to this book. By artistic, I first mean that the kind of observation of the natural world, of food, and of eating that characterizes this writing takes place in the realm of feeling. My second use of the term *artistic*, more in keeping with its usual usage, is the way in which the realm of feeling can be taken up in an act of making, which in this book refers primarily to cooking.

The artistic realm is the realm of feeling. Not emotion, and not personal feeling as "I feel this way or that way." Feeling is a way of knowing, a kind of cognition, not like the energetic reaction of emotion. We know things through feeling that cannot be known in any other way. Think of any of the arts—painting, music, dance, and all the rest. We know the world through these art forms in ways that cannot be known by intellect alone.

Artistic sensibility, however, is not confined to the well-known and structured arts. It can be applied to anything, especially the world of living beings. The living world is inherently feeling-filled. Feelings first belong to the living world, not to us personally. The feeling of the golden wheat in a field, the feeling of the rolling water over rocks, the feeling of the approach of spring, the feeling of the leafing of the plants, of the deep mystery of the root—these are the ways the world is described in this book.

The earth, nature, the cosmos is feeling-filled. And if we can attune our feeling life to the feeling qualities of the world, we become, or can become, scientists in the realm of feeling. We have thus combined art and science.

This book does exactly that. Doing so is inherently life-giving and life-supporting. And then, given this new science, we can imagine even more fully the extraordinary art of cooking. Cooking requires an imagination that can inwardly see all of the feeling processes of the natural world, in detail and not just in some vague, sentimental way. Further, the art of cooking requires the capacity to take the feeling elements of the natural world and not only intensify them, but combine them in new ways, ways unheard of in the natural world—ways that enhance nature, renew the qualities of nature, and equally take us into the quite invisible spiritual qualities of nature. This book works in this manner, and when you carefully read it, you will perceive the natural world anew, and your experience of eating will be completely different, enhanced, elevated.

If we follow through the act of eating to what then occurs in the body, we are taken into the realm of metabolism. In spiritual terms, the metabolism of the body concerns the element of the will. While the connection of metabolism, will, and the body is most apparent in the metabolism of the muscles—how we actually move and get around and do things in the world—it holds equally true for the processes of digestion, and also of reproduction. Not only are we nourished by food, but it determines the quality of our acts of will in the world.

We are not very aware of this connection until the body becomes once again more sensitive. Taking up the practices within this book does result in an increased bodily sensitivity, where it becomes possible to feel the relation between what and how we eat and the ways we relate with others.

While it might first sound somewhat incomprehensible, eating has moral ramifications. The spiritual approach to food taken in this book inevitably takes us in that direction and toward an understanding of planting, growing, cooking, and eating as an essential aspect of a spiritual path.

Robert Sardello, Ph.D.
Co-Director, The School of Spiritual Psychology

MY JOURNEY

As a teacher and counselor, I always strive to awaken wonder, reverence and enthusiasm toward the living world in young and old. The way to achieve planetary health and happiness is to bring alive, in every human heart, the glory and splendor of the world. To create a living relationship with the world is a most essential part of our diets today. As I marvel at the beauty and mysteries unfolding everywhere around me, I have come to know with certainty that real, natural foods reveal the splendor of the creative spirit. I also know for sure that what I cook and the way I prepare the meal is a continuation of these divine creative processes and have a profound impact in my life, as well as the life of humanity and the earth. For this understanding I am very grateful.

Wonder and reverence were awakened early in my life. I had the privilege to create an intimate relationship with nature from the time I was very young. I grew up north of Copenhagen in Denmark next to enchanting woods and wide-stretching fields, and a few miles from lapping ocean waves. My family lived in a community setting with a multitude of other families and children of all ages. As a baby and toddler, I napped in a carriage outside year-round. My kindergarten was in a forest with no physical address—the teacher strolled from door to door and picked up all the children along the way. We walked into the ever-changing woods and played among the fairies, trees and bushes. Our toys were rocks, sticks, moss, puddles, acorns and whatever else we found. With these natural toys there was no end for our creative imaginations. In nature we were free to be, move, and develop at our own pace.

When I was young in Denmark, television was not much of an option. Instead my sisters and I played with friends outside, rain or shine. It seemed like all weather was good weather when we were dressed well. We walked or biked a mile to school every day. After school the outside world and the seasonal changes in their entire splendor continued to frame all our games and activities.

After finishing high school I moved to Copenhagen to attend college. During that time I began to explore my individuality, freedom, and creativity as a young woman. Many questions came to birth in my heart. I had a feeling of longing—longing to know and to understand. Who was I? What was the source of my existence? I felt the stirring of a purpose in my life—what was it? While working as a systems analyst at IBM and later teaching computer science, my soul felt ignored and starved for real life. I felt a genuine unhappiness, and a deep sadness hovered around me. Although both jobs were interesting, challenging, and well paying, it wasn't what I was longing for. I was in emotional upheaval and despair.

This inner turmoil, the yearning to find answers to the questions I was carrying and the desire to really feel and experience life, led me on a new journey that embraced nature in a different way. Through the art of cooking I began consciously to reconnect and deepen my relationship with the world and nature—spiritually, creatively, and physically.

I enthusiastically devoted myself to the study of macrobiotics—*macro* meaning "great" and *biotic*, "life." I plunged into this all-embracing philosophy and began to recognize an interconnectedness with all beings and a spiritual world. My life changed completely. It began to make sense and have meaning. Every morning I awoke with joy and anticipation in my heart. My diet and lifestyle quickly transformed as my studies of the "great life" expanded to embrace oriental medicine, Buddhism, Sufism, and Iyengar Yoga. I began to teach, counsel, and cook for individuals and families as well as larger groups and summer camps.

I studied and worked with wonderful cooks and teachers of the macrobiotic way of life, guided by Aveline and Michio Kushi's compassionate and committed devotion to One Peaceful World. It was incredibly humbling to watch people, young and old, change to a lifestyle and diet in harmony with nature, restoring integrity to many parts of their lives, bringing their awareness to the spiritual nature and beauty around them while slowly reconnecting with their own personal gifts and purposes. These changes completely reversed their destiny. I had friends and clients who were bedridden, in incredible pain, and on the threshold of dying. Through the life changes they made, they regained their health and vitality. It totally redirected their future. It was then my husband, Wil, and I wrote and published a series of 10 cookbooks on health and diet. For many years we taught and traveled together in Europe and the United States, cooking, gardening, and practicing various healing arts with extraordinary people.

We explored the art of cooking from different cultures and how these cultures connected to the universal life forces, the healing arts, and spirituality. I came to appreciate how food, cooking, and lifestyles related to the health and development of the consciousness of humanity. I learned much from wise old country women residing in the remote mountains of Scandinavia and isolated islands of the Caribbean, in the central planes of old Yugoslavia and the coastal regions of Greece. I worked with many creative, inspiring women during that time, among them Wendy Esko, Susanne Jensen, Karen Stephan, Karin Schrøder-Schmidt, Gabrielle Kushi, Lili Just Møller, Lisbeth Tordendahl, Regine Carr, and wild, passionate women such as Susun Weed and Barbara Berger. I also became familiar with hundreds of awesome teachers and cooks through books and magazines. I am immensely grateful to every one of them.

A few years after my husband and I moved to the country in the midwestern United States, I became a class teacher at Pleasant Ridge Waldorf School. I was delighted to live on a farm while teaching young children. It gave me a great opportunity to develop my relationship with nature as well as discover more of the mystery of life, human development, and the holiness of education. I was graced with an exceptional group of children whom I led through the elementary years from first through eighth grade. The magnificent Waldorf curriculum, created by philosopher, scientist, and artist Rudolf Steiner, motivated me to further embark on biodynamic gardening and anthroposophical medicine.

After graduating my class I mentored other grade teachers. I taught in a Waldorf-inspired high school, working with groups of teenagers who were searching for answers to some of the same questions I had at their age. I was able to share with them my enthusiasm for life in the areas of agriculture, projective geometry, mathematics, painting, and life skills.[1]

I currently teach in a Waldorf kindergarten. Inspired by my own childhood experiences in nature and Helle Heckmann's forest kindergarten in Denmark, I bring the young children outside as much as possible where they are free to move and develop naturally. I delight in the life on our biodynamic farm and carry on my studies of healing and medicine. As I continue to offer natural health counseling in person and by phone across the country, I have come to honor even more the challenges and holiness of illness and health. My visions of the future include a school where the *living art of cooking* is explored by many and supports everyone in meeting their destiny and fulfilling their dreams.

---

[1] *I Find My Star*, by Tamara Slayton, Linda Knodle, and Anne-Marie Fryer Wiboltt.

Numerous incredible teachers and mentors helped and inspired me on my journey. I am very thankful to all of them and especially Tamara Slayton, John Gardner, Leo Klein and Sharon Lester. Another extraordinary person is the founder and co-director of the School of Spiritual Psychology, Robert Sardello. His brilliant work radiates into all areas of my life and breathes through the pages of this book.

I would like to further acknowledge and express my deepest appreciation to friends and family who helped make this book possible, and especially to Wil Fryer for his wholehearted support; my mother, Elisabeth Wiboltt, for her loving interest; Robert Sardello and Cheryl Sardello-Sander as well as Goldenstone Press for their dedicated commitment to publishing this book; Leo Klein for his professional artistic advice, encouraging comments, and inspiring artwork; Parker Forsell, Carol Kozminski, Jo Ann Killen, and Loma Huh for enthusiastic editorial work; Richard Wehrman for his beautiful, professional design; Donna Simmons for her guiding light; and last but not least the women of the Golden Rose Garden: Sorel Haruf, Diana Horan, Julee Sander, Jessie Rogers, Sarah Kamin, Kim Snyder-Vine, Laura Radefeld, and Susanne Zipperlein, for their passionate support.

INTRODUCTION

A diet of wholesome, locally grown seasonal foods lays a foundation for clear, open, and living thinking, a healthy inner life of feeling, and a strong will to fulfill our life's tasks and purposes. A strong, flexible body with a healthy inner life is the chalice and instrument for true listening and receiving of soul/spirit wisdom.

If we want to answer the question of what we should eat and which foods are good for us, we each have to enter into this chalice and listen deeply to our own true knowing. We alone know the answers to the question. We can learn to cultivate this inner knowing. It can be sensed in a real bodily way. If we pause for a minute and in silence connect with our inner being, we can clearly feel whether we are weighted down or not grounded enough. With practice we can sense what is making us feel heavy or flighty and what dietary and lifestyle changes can help change this feeling.

When we enter into this knowing, which is more in the realm of the heart than in the mind, we are present to the wisdom of the world. We experience how our body and soul belong to the activities of the earth and cosmos. As we attend to these activities with genuine interest, we come to know life and the universal in every creation. Gratitude, wonder and awe open us to a place of receptivity to the world and its processes and rhythms. Creating beautiful, nourishing meals that resonate with the wisdom and harmony in nature is like living our lives as an open, unfolding work of art.

Many people today perceive the food they eat as a certain amount of calories or substances such as minerals, vitamins, fats, proteins, and carbohydrates. This technical information is useful in some ways but at the same time gives a very limited and narrow experience of the meal in front of us. When we see the world and the food we eat mainly in materialistic, scientific units, we neglect or eliminate beauty and soul. Our hearts are robbed of awe and reverence toward all we are given as nourishment. These feelings are only allowed to emerge when we begin to perceive the meal completely differently.

Cooking for the Love of the World is a book that encourages everyone to develop a new and fresh relationship with the world through the art of cooking. The living art of cooking, as described here, awakens wonder for the abundance of nature in her beauty and polarities. It shows that the food we eat is created by active life forces imbued with special qualities and has different properties that we consciously can make use of in our daily and medicinal cooking. We learn to continue nature's creative processes in our own kitchen and to create artistic, well-balanced meals in harmony with each season. We are guided to the understanding that every selection of food, every cutting style, and every cooking method has a different qualitative effect on our whole being, including how we feel and think. But this living art of cooking is more than an enjoyable, health-giving, creative activity; it is also an important aspect of any inner path of spiritual development.

Cooking for the Love of the World reaches toward the divine within nature. It leads us on a path of wonder, gratitude and reverence. Because the book helps us redirect our gaze toward the processes of what is to come, it involves our own destiny and the destiny of the world. Working with this book will bring clarity in our spiritual life, enliven our thinking, warm our feelings, and promote health and happiness. Our transformed inner life and good health will, in turn, enrich humanity and the world. This living art of cooking is the answer to the materialistic threats of our time and restoring the dignity of life.

The book contains many exercises or explorations that will engage the will, create heart-felt understanding, and enliven the imagination and thinking. Realities come about through what lives. When these explorations are accompanied by true feelings, then the content of this book will no longer remain only intellectual understanding. Instead it will awaken spiritual knowledge, without which we cannot bring about real change in our life. We will come to experience an inner radiance, which will permeate the depth of our being and everyone around us.

I believe that this inner radiance or spiritual light is an achievement; it doesn't "just happen." It begins with experiencing the feeling of gratitude and wonder. It begins with a real, intimate relationship with nature and the bounty of food with which she graces us. The food we eat is created within her rhythms. These rhythms—the cycle of the day, the year, and the hemispheric seasonal changes of the earth—belong to the life processes of the earth as well as to the spirit of the earth, because the spirit of the earth lives and creates within these life processes. In my imagination the spirit of the earth is the spirit of Love. *Cooking for the Love of the World* encourages us to awaken to the spirit of the earth, the spirit of Love.

RHYTHMS IN THE WORLD

We live in a world of constant change. Day transforms into night and summer into winter. Every morning a new day is birthed, and every evening it dies away for the night to be born. The moon becomes full, wanes, and disappears for three days before it reappears anew. The seasons flow into each other, each giving way to the next. Blessed with these changes, no two days are alike.

When we are attentive to the subtle differences in our daily lives, we discover that the vegetation changes during the course of the year and that colors have different hues in the changing light of the day. Shadows lengthen and shorten, the humidity fluctuates through the seasons, and the wind whirls around at times softly, at times vigorously. The temperature rises and falls, and different scents present themselves under different conditions.

We begin to feel life itself—the warmth and cold of the air, the wetness and flexibility of soil, and the hardness and inflexibility of wood and rocks. With all our senses we feel the earth breathe and change. We enter into the blue of the sky, let it pervade our whole being, and feel the reverence that embraces the earth. We look to the starry realms of night and are filled with joy and veneration at being near our true origin.

Being present to life itself, we come to know and appreciate deeply that life emerges in cosmic cycles and rhythms. This discovery was to me incredibly significant. My awareness went to my breathing rhythms, the rhythm of my heart and digestion. I noticed that my menstrual cycle had a rhythm of its own, yet it was directly connected with the cycle of the moon. I observed how I lived with the rhythms of the sun in my sleeping and waking life, and how seven-year cycles seemed to guide my life. I began to experience myself as a human being of rhythms. The sense of interconnectedness I had with the cosmos awoke feelings of joy, gratitude,

 Explore

In what ways do you experience yourself as a being of rhythm?

and anticipation within me. I slowly came to the understanding that in working with these cycles and rhythms consciously, I had an opportunity to create in concert with the cosmos and really meet my destiny instead of sleepily going through the day, letting life's circumstances blow me this way and that.

Practically, in terms of my daily lifestyle and eating habits, this meant that I could quite consciously create meals that harmonized with the cosmic and earthly rhythms. This was a much different experience than being pushed and pulled by my sensory cravings or my intellect, which most often led to unhappiness and uneasiness. Instead I could create healthy eating habits in rhythm with nature that laid the foundation for clarity of thought, stability of emotions, strength of motivation, and a healthy sense of well-being. When I experienced challenges, I had the clarity to arrange my life in such a way that I could take the steps I needed and receive the gifts that these difficulties often brought.

Living harmoniously as a being of rhythm within the rhythms in nature begins with living into the daily and seasonal changes in a conscious way. These changes are related to the revolution of the earth as it rhythmically spirals in an ocean of light belonging to the sun and the many stars. What a marvel to bring this picture alive in the imagination! To wonder at the unbelievable precision with which this rotation happens in the bosom of life-sustaining light will keep us in continual awe and reverence.

THE YEARLY SEASONAL CYCLES

Springtime is the season of new beginnings. As the sun climbs higher in the sky, we sense the earth exhaling anew ascending currents of life forces. We experience deeply the outward, upward growth and the opening feeling of renewal as a contrast to the withdrawing of life forces in winter. Through the interplay of the sun and the earth, nature's power of growth intensifies, and millions of tons of leaves and grasses are brought forth within weeks. The new life and vitality of spring fill us with jubilation and hope.

In summer the earth is breathing out its life forces completely. The sun is at its highest, bathing our world in warmth and light. The air feels full and expanded. The growth processes, begun in the spring, are now at their peak, ripening and maturing. The gardens and fields yield a cornucopia of fresh fruits and vegetables. The magical moods of summer penetrate us with enthusiasm and warmth while we dream the midsummer's dreams.

 Explore

Express the moods of each season through poetry, painting, or drawing.

With autumn approaching, the days mellow. We experience the sun's weakening influence on earth and the softening of the light. As the sun withdraws from the hemisphere, the earth mother inhales with certainty the life forces back into her womb. Temperatures fall and growth processes slow down. Leaves fall from their branches and seeds drop to the ground. We bring the harvest to the root cellar and put the garden to rest. As winter draws nearer, our thinking crystallizes, courage builds up, and our inner light strengthens.

The drawing in of life forces that began in fall continues through the beginning of winter and is completed as solstice approaches. These forces condense and stay active below the soil while on the surface of the ground everything seems lifeless and asleep. The sun is above the horizon for the shortest time, but the moon rises higher, staying in the night sky for many more hours than in the summer. In our garden, seeds cuddle cozily under a blanket of snow, waiting for spring to arrive. We snuggle closer to the hearth as winter guides us into a quiet, inward mood of solitude and contemplation.

THE RHYTHMS OF THE DAY

Morning resembles springtime, where the world awakens and stirs with new life. We begin to feel the upward drawing forces of levity. In the eastern sky, the first light presses night away ever so gently. It is as if the goddess of dawn, in colors of magenta, is heralding the birth of the sun. The dark, almost black horizon softens as the goddess draws after her a golden veil. What a magnificent moment when the first speck of light shows. As the earth awakens, lifting and breathing out its life forces, we too experience with certainty the flow of creativity.

At midday the sun reaches its highest peak. Gazing down from on high, the sun creates fewer and shorter shadows and less dramatic colors. Everything is bathed in bright light. Flowers and leaves turn toward the sun to receive the strong light, warmth, and forces from the cosmos. At this time of day we inwardly experience the delight and joy of creating.

Toward evening the earth draws in again. As the golden sun descends, it changes into its red garments. The horizon darkens; soon nature and most of its creations will be resting. Dewdrops condense, flowers close their delicate petals, and birds settle in the trees, singing their last songs to the evening. We feel the pull of gravity, the downward-moving forces, as we prepare to go to bed. We reflect on our day and harvest the experiences we gained. The stars make their appearance and rekindle awe at the magnificent universe we are a part of.

A WISDOM-FILLED WORLD

Let us now walk into an autumn day and gaze at a field of wheat swaying like the sea in the wind under the blue and red evening sky. Mature and ready for harvest, its golden radiance sets the landscape aglow. Get closer and observe the tall, strong, erect stem of each wheat grass. At the very top, tightly packed, sits a cluster of kernels, each pointing toward the celestial sky.

Feel the hardness of the grains. Bite into them and taste the raw young wheat kernels. Smell the freshness of these golden treasures that have sustained humanity for ages. Who produces these wonderful golden grains? How and by what is this field of grains being created? Standing next to the field we get the feeling that along with the world of visible matter (the leaves, stalks, and grains), invisible forces are at work in the process of growing this field of wheat.

If we hold the wheat kernel in our hands and "see" its potential—what it is to become—we will grasp a little of this invisible world. We will see with our mind's eye the brown seeds planted in the moist fertile ground, how they sprout, setting down roots and shooting up the first young green leaves. If we continue to imagine the green wheat grasses developing into a mature golden field of wheat with withering stalks and leaves, then we have clearly seen the processes of growth and decay. When we practice this way of seeing, we develop a skill or an organ of perception with which we can perceive the invisible forces at work in nature. In this way it becomes possible to get to know the invisible world through clear imaginative thinking.

Let us now hold a cabbage in our hands and open ourselves to a sense of wonder and awe at what we see. This might be difficult at first. One way to connect with the feeling of wonder is to create a poem of our impressions about the cabbage or have a kind of "conversation" with the cabbage. Observe it in details. Open all your senses and notice what they tell you. How does the cabbage feel in your hands? Is it cold or warm? Is it heavy or light? Is it symmetrical? Does it have a delicate smell or taste? What does it sound like when you break off a leaf? What are you experiencing holding this cabbage?

Become aware that when you are looking at this cabbage with all your senses open in wonder, awe, and astonishment, a feeling of reverence surges through you—a reverence that is new and fresh and completely unexpected. If we can stay with this feeling, we will begin to see something of the wisdom within and around the cabbage. We will clearly experience that some forces allowed this beautiful cabbage to appear and motivated it into being.

It is a great gift to the world when we begin to see the creative life forces and the interweaving of these forces in all creations. Once we experience the world in this new way, we enliven a true imagination that is beyond intellectual understanding. Then a genuine feeling for the invisible wisdom in nature arises in us and the experience becomes a real spiritual sensing. Our souls begin at once to be transformed, and so does this invisible world in which we participate.

CREATIVE LIFE FORCES

Looking at a carrot, we usually only notice the outer manifestations of matter. In reality what we see is the physical outcome of what has been created by invisible spiritual forces. The carrot itself is an activity produced by invisible, creative life forces—an activity that is constantly changing and metamorphosing,

In order to see the activity of a carrot plant and the creative life forces forming it, let us imagine a tiny seed sprouting and growing into a lovely, vermilion-red, sweet, crisp carrot with green tops. We observe first the root of the carrot, growing downward vertically around its center. Compared with its leaves the root is dense with matter. The carrot tops, by contrast, are drawn upward toward the periphery, spreading out horizontally. They are lighter, thinner, with an almost lacy look. Already we notice two opposite, yet complementary, forces at work that qualitatively are completely different. One is the downward-spiraling centripetal force which is often referred to as gravity, and the other is the upward-spiraling centrifugal force known as levity.

But what is gravity? Is it a force in the earth pulling the root of the carrot downward toward the earth's center, or forces from the cosmic heavens pushing down? What about levity? Is it a cosmic force drawing or sucking the leaves upward, unfolding them as they reach to meet the light? Or is levity a force pushing from the earth,

Explore

Imagine that you hold in one hand a seed of a sunflower and in the other an exact clay imitation of that seed. To the physical sight they look exactly alike. Imagine in detail the seed of the sunflower sprout, mature, wither and decay. What is missing in the clay imitation? Why doesn't it sprout?

pressing the leaves outward and upward in a spiral, centrifugal movement? Let us keep these questions in our hearts for a moment. For now, notice that the interplay of the invisible formative forces creates a polarity. One aspect spirals downward and has a relationship to density, matter, and heaviness connected to earthly forces. The other spirals upward and is peripheral by nature. It has a relationship to nondensity, nonmatter, and lightness, connected to cosmic or celestial forces.

Where do these forces originate? We usually view physical space and matter as having a center, a point connected to gravity, the earth's force. But what about the forces we call levity? Could they be connected to the periphery, the cosmos?

Imagine that there are forces originating at infinity and coming in toward the planet. Whereas the point-centered force of gravity is centric and contractive in nature, the force originating at infinity is peripheral and expansive.

It is difficult to imagine inward-moving forces originating at infinity. Some years ago when I worked at a Waldorf-inspired high school, I taught a class called projective geometry [2] that introduced this principle. With its roots reaching back into the 1500s, this beautiful realm of geometry is today considered by scientists to be the seed of new directions in all the sciences relating to living nature, including food and medicine. I remember how I rejoiced when I discovered projective geometry. It provided not only the exactitude and clarity we find in the realm of mathematics but also a real scientific imagination of the formative creative life. With its scientific indications that two complementary forces operate in the world (the earth-centered as well as the force centered at and coming from infinity), this geometry creates real pictures of how all living and moving forms emerge artfully from a self-ordering chaos. Although projective geometry is fairly simple, based on direct observations and practical applications using only planes, lines, and points, I recall how the students struggled with the idea of two qualitatively different forces active in the world. In their youth they had already become accustomed to thinking, as the rest of us, of the world being governed by one creative force, the one of gravity.

Knowing how our ordinary thinking is being challenged, let us continue and picture these peripheral forces moving in from realms of cosmic space, creating spatial forms from without. Just as a circle or a sphere can be drawn from a center with the radius being an equal distance from that point, or can be drawn by drawing the planes or tangents on the circumference, so can all living forms be seen as being created from within as well as being enveloped by creative forces from without.

 Explore

Draw a circle from a central point. The distance from the center point to any other point on the circle will be the same.

On another piece of paper draw the same size circle, this time from planes (tangents) originating from the periphery. Do you have a different experience when drawing this circle?

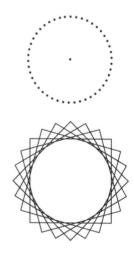

[2] *The Plant Between the Sun and the Earth* by Olive Whitcher; *Projective Geometry* by Olive Witcher; *Mathematics in the Classroom* by Amos Franceschelli.

The physical center, held by gravity or the earth force, draws the peripheral and ethereal life force in toward itself. These enveloping creative forces create a sphere infinitely receptive to cosmic forces. They leave a kind of hollow to be "filled" with substance or matter. Modern scientists say that the familiar physical and chemical laws we have been taught in school are excellent to measure and weigh anything physical with precision. We can calculate the distance to the moon and measure minute amounts of minerals in a laboratory carrot. However, when it comes to understanding and explaining how the carrot plant itself grew toward the light (against gravity), these sciences, as we know them, are insufficient. Metamorphosis and transformation in the living world can only be understood, they say, as a result of two invisible and qualitatively different forces; the earth-centered and the peripheral or cosmic.

We can imagine every living thing created by the interplay between the polarities of the point-centered, more fixed and finite earth space, and the peripheral, flexible, open-ended, ever moving and infinite cosmic space. Were the forces of gravity to operate alone, every material body would collapse into its own center or toward the center of the earth. That does not happen because the ethereal, cosmic life forces seek to bestow their life-awakening qualities. And the ethereal cosmic forces do not simply follow their natural cosmic tendency and float away or dissipate into the periphery, but are drawn to and offer their life forces inwardly toward the living, growing center.

We can think of infinity as existing as a potential in the pure light of thought—not as a realm in a far-distant place but a spiritual, creative realm, the ever-present source of everything. Thinking then can become the interpreter of living phenomena, without leaning to mysticism, and awaken a new perception of living forms and space.

Imbued with this clear imaginative thinking we can now transcend the old picture we held of a plant growing out into the space around it, being pushed upward from the ground or thrust like an arrow into the space. We can instead imagine that the plant unfolds from the growing tip and is sucked or drawn upward by forces connected to the realm of pure light, the stars and constellations. Picture these cosmic forces endowing each plant with its varied qualities as they draw and spiral the physical substances outward. And imagine that around the plant is, not an empty space, but a life-filled space of vital life forces.

NATURE BEINGS IN THE WORLD

Cultures with deep roots in the past recognize that the whole world, with all its delicate life processes, is created by earthly forces and by forces coming in from the starry cosmic world. Indigenous peoples understand these forces to be moved by beings in nature. The presence of these living beings is to be found within every shimmering star and constellation, every moving cloud, roaring thunder, and the growth and decay of all living phenomena. This relationship between the people and nature beings is expressed through cultural rituals, stories, songs, and many other art forms.

The whole natural world is, to these cultures, a manifestation of the activities of spiritual beings. Some specific beings are called elementals. They are known to condense the invisible life forces, raying in from the cosmos, into physical substance. Therefore matter is understood not to be fixed but to manifest as four activities or transformations; earth (solids), water (liquids), air (gases), and fire (warmth).

Everything solid or condensed with finite shape is formed by nature beings of the earth, known by some as gnomes. Minerals, pinches of salt, roots, ice cubes, and the bark of trees are examples of the hardened nature of earth substance. These solids have definite independent forms and are influenced strongly by the earth forces we have come to know as gravity. They are the most rigid manifestations of life.

Liquids are influenced more by cosmic forces than the solids. We have all observed how water runs low but as vapor and mist it is lifted up high. The downward-flowing rivers as well as the upward-running saps of leaves and trees are in the liquid state of water. Fluids lie between the solids and the gases. They have no form; the vessels in which they are contained give them shape. Within water and liquids many chemical interactions and transformations take place. Water nymphs or undines are believed to dwell in lakes and rivers.

Sylphs, the beings inhabiting air, move within all gases and everything expanding upward and outward in all directions. Gases are completely emancipated from the condensing earthly forces and totally opposite solids. They are without form and imbued with light, active cosmic forces. The rising of steam and smoke, the bobbles in rising dough, and the delicate scents of apple blossoms are lifted by these beings of air.

Warmth has an even finer substantiality than air. It belongs to the activity of the fire sprites. This ethereal nature of warmth is so delicate and subtle that it is

 Explore

Take a rock in your hand. Can you, in your imagination, see that once the rock was fluid and before that a gaseous substance? Imagine that the gaseous material proceeded from the spiritual. Did the rock become solid only in the course of time?

Do you sense the nature beings that are responsible for these transformations of matter? Feel the presence of the beings of the rock you hold. How is this experience different from just looking at it and admiring it?

on both sides of the threshold of the spiritual and material world. In the realm of warmth, the material world with its three-dimensional space can be left entirely. It is the nature of fire to expand and dissipate toward the spiritual and ethereal as well as condense toward the perceptible, material world.

These four active transformations of matter are in constant movement, interconnecting and permeating each other. We know water best as a fluid, yet if we bring it to a boil it evaporates into the air as steam, as a gas. If instead of heating water we cool it down so that it freezes, it takes on a solid form and becomes ice. The solid nature of ice is brought out of water as liquid. It disappears again when it is changed back into a fluid.

In this spectacular imagination of nature, all physical matter is condensed warmth or pure spirit light. The origin of matter is to be found in a realm entirely different than matter itself. Out of this realm the spiritual individualizes and manifests itself in multiple forms of existence. Matter is not fixed, as we are accustomed to think, but is in constant movement and can be experienced as activities created by spirit beings.

This dynamic interaction between the polarities of contracting and expanding forces, of solidity and ethereal warmth, exists everywhere in nature. Observe for example how the elemental beings work together in the creation of a kohlrabi. Experience the firmness of the grounding life-sustaining root so connected to the earthly forces. The leaves of the kohlrabi feel much less solid than the root. They are saturated with water. Within the juicy leaves, substances are constantly created and transformed. The white and purple flowers that appear later in the season are even less earthy and more insubstantial and delicate than the leaves. They are of the sweet-scented, light-permeated air, nearly dissipating into the cosmic warmth.

These various, very creative, elemental beings are ethereal beings living in the invisible world. They are familiar to most of us only through poetry, folk stories, and fairy tales. We hear about the hardworking gnomes walking in and out of the soil, trolls abiding in the depth of the mountains, frost giants roaming the land, beautiful water nymphs playing in the stream, flower fairies of the fields, and fire sprites flickering in the warmth of summer solstice. The lovely image-rich fairy tales we find all over the world speak in living pictures of what was once understood to be spiritual and active in nature. These tales give us the feeling that we are everywhere immersed in and surrounded by a living, wisdom-filled world.

THE LIVING WORLD TODAY

To the people of the past, spiritual beings brought life into the whole sphere of the earth. From spiritual light and warmth, they created and maintained the physical world. Spiritual beings fashioned this marvelous, beautiful, living world that we experience every day. What happened to these beings? Where are they now?

In our modern society we have lost the feeling and understanding of a living world and separated ourselves completely from it. We have become very materialistic, relying mostly on what we can see, weigh, and measure. The laws that govern the physical, solid world of matter have weighed us down heavily.

Today we are not expected to live on beliefs of the past or to follow old rituals. Rather each one of us is asked to research and create for ourselves ways to relate to the living world of nature that are both scientific and filled with spirit. It is of utmost importance for the development of all life, and especially humanity, that we regain a genuine experience of the living, active spirit that was once so evident.

To really understand the essence of nutrition and foods, as well as the source of all living phenomena as it transforms and metamorphoses, requires the courage to re-imagine what we have been taught in traditional schools. We must bring to consciousness a view other than the purely material we have been given so far in our education and nourish an imagination that offers radically different ways of experiencing living phenomena, spatial forms, and space itself. Our very well-developed intellectual knowledge of the physical world cannot reach into the foundation of nature and our own existence.

In order to gain real insight into this world of nature and food, we must first trust our own direct perceptual observations. Through practice we will become able to perceive the invisible forces, which cause living substances to rise upward, visibly overcoming the earthly forces known as gravity. When we perceive these forces and consciously immerse ourselves within the breathing rhythms of growth and decay everywhere around us, we come to experience with certainty that everything is continually in a process of becoming. Then we come to know food and cooking as qualitative processes, renewed and regenerated inward from the celestial realms, instead of merely material substances made of minerals, fats, protein, and carbohydrates.

 Explore

Take a walk in nature and create in your imagination a picture of the earth as a living being. Sense how the earth breathes. Listen to the sap in the trees. Follow the clouds in the sky. Where are they going? Where did they originate?

How does it feel to be walking within living presences? Did your stride change?

THE CYCLE AND
RHYTHMS OF A PLANT

When I taught the natural sciences in the middle grades of the Waldorf school, I was given no formula or textbook to follow. Rather I was asked to develop the pedagogical curriculum out of an understanding of the human being as body, soul, and spirit. Philosopher, scientist, and artist Rudolf Steiner gave the guidelines for this understanding of the human being, called *anthroposophy*. It was my job as a teacher to develop lessons that I had worked through myself, lessons that would strengthen the students' capacity for objectivity, enliven their thinking, deepen their interest in the world, and be relevant and meaningful in life.

I found great assistance in Goethe's scientific works grounded in practicality. Goethe laid the foundation for the understanding that reality can be grasped through clear imaginative thinking and accurate objective perception. Although not commonly known today, his methods led to completely new insights into nature and the world of plants. Goethe was the first scientist to suggest an archetypal life cycle of plants—what we have come to know as the development, gestures, and forms typical of most plants. Much of what is offered in this book is attributed to his way of observing and thinking *with*, instead of *about*, the world of nature.

Before we take a look at the growth processes of the archetypal plant, let us place it in connection to the seasonal rhythms. In temperate regions, the entire plant covering of the earth breathes rhythmically between the summer activity of growth and blossoming and the winter activity of decaying and rest. This activity resembles the waking and sleeping activity of animals and human beings, except that the plant covering in each hemisphere is always awake one half of the year and asleep the other half. The conditions of "waking and sleeping" move around the earth spatially. Just as the sun at daybreak calls us away from sleep, so does the sun lure out the plant covering of the earth in the spring and summer. Although each plant awakens at different times throughout the year and has a definite rhythm of its own, we can through keen observation experience a clear life cycle, universal to all plants, related to the cycle of the year.

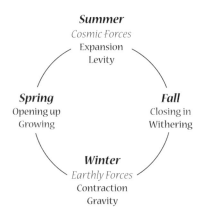

If we plant a tiny seed of leaf lettuce in the moist soil, we can observe how the leaves slowly begin to grow. They spiral outward and up, ascending, and at the same time reach horizontally toward the light. The plant is all growth and expansion until the forming of the buds from which the delicate white or yellow blossoms appear. Within the flowering blossoms begin the condensing, descending forces and inward growth processes of reproduction. The fruits develop in the heart of the flowers, protecting the very condensed mature seeds. The plant withers and the seeds drop to the ground for the cycle to start over.

Such a cycle of expansion and contraction, known as the life cycle of the archetypal plant, is typical of most plants. It is like an idea or a spiritual reality or being that manifests in a plant through growth and decay. Much like an idea that begins as a thought and is later realized in the physical world, the spiritual reality or being connects with physical matter and becomes perceptible to our senses. As the plant withers and fades away, leaving nothing but the seeds, this spiritual reality or being of the plant withdraws into the cosmic realm.

What follows is a description of the archetypal plant in further detail and an imagination of how the polarities of the lighter, peripheral cosmic forces and the denser, heavier earthly forces work magically through contraction and expansion in the different parts of the plant that we enjoy as food.

GROUNDING ROOTS

The root has its life in the moist soil. It hugs the earth and penetrates into its dark, cool, watery realm. Here it grows vertically down while simultaneously branching

out. The forces of the earth support this beginning process of a new plant. The root anchors and sustains the plant with life. Without the foothold in the solid earth there would be no plant.

The roots are very similar to the soil wherein they grow. As the earth, they contain many salts and minerals. Roots are very firm and tough. They are primarily a product of densifying and contracting earth forces. The stronger these forces are at work, the harder, more rigid and solid the roots become. The cosmic forces, too, are present in the root and the new shoots but they have given themselves over to the physical and earthly realm. Even though the leaves and flowers of perennial plants wither and decay, their roots sleep in the ground through the winter. When spring returns, new life sprouts forth from the wintered roots.

The earthly, downward-moving, strong forces are the primary creators of all roots. Within the root family of vegetables, some are more strongly connected to the grounding earthly forces than others. For example, the burdock root spirals downward, penetrating powerfully and deeply into the ground two to three feet, whereas other roots like beets grow more round just below the surface of the soil and are therefore influenced by more expansive forces compared to the deep-reaching burdock root.

Have you noticed how you feel after eating root vegetables? Do you feel more grounded and clearer in your thinking?

MAGIC BETWEEN ROOT AND STEM

It is an amazing experience to observe in detail the different parts of plants. Look at a new carrot with its top and pay attention to the place where the root and stem meet. Notice how different the growth forces are of the root and of the leaves. One creates the upward-growing lacy green tops, the other the downward-reaching compact root. What happens there between these two forces of growth?

On the base where the top is connected with the root, the forces intensify immensely. At this place the centripetal downward-spiraling movement changes into a centrifugal upward spiraling force. And if we continue to study the root and the top a little closer, we find the inside core of the carrot root has become the outer peripheral fibrous layers of the leafy greens. What is happening between the root and stem is a complete turning upside down and inside out. The vermilion red carrot and the deep green top belong together and complement each other like night and day. The place where the root and stem meet is the threshold between two worlds.

When we clean roots we make sure to trim neatly around these transformative parts of the vegetables and include them in our meal or soup stocks.

LIGHT LEAFY GREENS

All leafy greens, compared to roots, have a closer relationship to the cosmic forces. These forces lift the plants out of their earthly gravity, in an expansive upward and outward movement, into a wealth of multi-shaped, individual, beautiful leaves.

Take a look at a common plant, such as a blossoming stinging nettle. Beginning at the root, allow your eyes to follow one leaf to the other. Notice the ordered, rhythmical progression of leaf after leaf around the stem.

Observe the wavelike movement of the foliage. At the bottom of the plant the leaves are small and round. Around the middle of the stem the leaves are larger and more differentiated. Directly under the flowers the leaves get smaller again but are now elongated and pointed. These more leggy top leaves are announcing the arrival of the flowers—something coming from the future! Sense how the archetypal, spiritual reality or being expresses itself in the physical development and growth of the leaves. It feels as if there are forces active within this growth process that are both universal and yet very individual for each plant.[3]

The leaves are flat and extend horizontally toward the light. Within each green leaf two opposite invisible movements take place: Each leaf breathes in the subtle elements of light-filled air and evaporates the upward-drawn moisture from the ground. One movement is directed toward the surroundings, the periphery. Here sap and water evaporate on the surface of the leaf. The other is the movement from the periphery toward the plant, where airy gases and substances are absorbed by the leaves. This marvelous breathing process allows, inside the watery juices of the leaf and stem, substances to be created and biochemical interactions to take place.

It is interesting to compare leafy greens of different plants to one another. Notice how the cosmic expanding forces are stronger in greens that are lighter and have a more outreaching character than those that grow more contracted, formed, and differentiated leaves.

Look at the different greens you have in the kitchen, such as lettuce, collards, kale, Chinese cabbages, turnips greens, spinach, or watercress. Observe the upward-

 Explore

Make your own medicinal tinctures. Gather the desired fresh parts of the plant— for example, nettle leaves, flowering stalks of motherwort, dandelion root, valerian root, echinacea, etc. Cut roots and stalks fine and pack them loosely, each herb in separate glass jar. Cover the plant material with 100 proof alcohol. Let the jar sit in a cool, dark place for 6 weeks. Strain the tincture. Use 10-15 drops in a glass of water when needed.

---

[3] *New Eyes for Plants* by Margaret Colquhoun and Axel Ewald; *The Plant Between the Sun and the Earth* by Olive Whitcher.

growing movement of the leaves, hardly influenced by forces of gravity. Have you noticed how you feel after eating leafy greens? Do you feel lighter and more outward-reaching, perhaps even breathing deeper and more rhythmically?

INTENSIFICATION BETWEEN STEM AND FLOWER

As we bring our attention to a plant that is about to flower, we discover that the elongated green leaves at the very top look as if they are gradually withdrawing. The upward growing stem appears to come to a halt. Tiny leaves begin to form a bud that slowly swells, then opens outward horizontally and symmetrically. Now once more, as between the root and the stem, a total intensification and transformation is taking place. The stem seems to be turned upside down and inside out in the creation of the flower. This newly created blossom is so light and heavenly, there is nothing earthly about it.

MAGNIFICENT FLOWER

It is awe-inspiring to observe a small bud transform into a magnificent flower. As the blossom opens ever so gently, it gives the feeling of enveloping a holy space or sphere. In the warm, light-filled air this delicate, lovely chalice tenderly unfolds to the glory of the cosmos.

Sense how the cosmic peripheral forces stream inward toward the plant. So active in the summer's heat, they lift the delicate substances of the flower up and outward. It is as if the blossom is allowed to pour itself out into the universe in brilliant colors, nectars, and delicate pollens. Still higher and higher they lift the finer substances of the flower essence into the ethereal fragrances that pleasantly draw the buzzing insects.

As the substances of the flower are lifted into the air, something else is beginning to happen simultaneously. While the whole plant is growing it is spiraling up and outward to meet the light. Now the growth processes begin their inward and downward journey.

Whenever possible gather edible flowers such as golden dandelion flowers, blue borage blossoms, carmine red nasturtiums or golden yellow calendula. Look at them through a magnifying glass and observe the spectacular details. Decorate your meal with these heavenly blossoms.

❀ *Explore*

Look at the blossoming squash plant in the summer. See it sprouting in the spring, bearing fruit in the fall, and its "lifeless" seeds resting in the ground through the cold winter. Try to perceive the whole plant by being present to all its life stages at once.

HEAVY SWEETNESS OF FRUITS

As the earthly forces again become more influential in the development of the plant, the fruits grow bigger and stronger to protect the developing seeds. The fruits take on magnificent shapes, colors, and textures that differentiate varieties from one another. The heaviness of the fruits brings the seeds to the ground so that within the womb of the earth the seeds will, in the following season, attract new life forces for the cycle to start over.

The word fruit most often brings to the imagination sweet cherries and apples, but many vegetable plants also produce fruits. The fruit of the plant is the part that embraces the developing seeds, which includes many vegetables such as olives, zucchinis, and squashes. Interesting variations are the raspberry, in which each little seed is enveloped separately, and the strawberry, which creates its seeds on the outside.

SUN-RIPENED SEEDS

Protected by the enveloping fruit, the seeds can slowly begin to ripen. In the abundance of sunlight and warmth, the seeds mature and get ready to winter. They are the very last to develop before the plant withers and decays. The seed is the culmination of the beginning and the end, of dying and becoming. It is as if the seed condenses the cosmic warmth, light, movement, and life it needs in readiness for the next spring's germination. These little rich and oily gems are highly concentrated and full of potential vitality.

There are many different culinary and medicinal seeds and nuts, such as sesame seeds, flax seeds, pumpkin seeds, sunflower seeds, hazelnuts, chestnuts, and walnuts. Notice their high oil content. Have you ever wondered where this oil actually comes from? The oils and the germs of the seeds are protected by a shell or hull. As soon as the shell of the nut is cracked the seeds start to decay and the oils become rancid.

Try to sprout a few sunflower seeds and observe them as they grow. What happens to the seeds after they are planted? They swell, metamorphose, and die away. The seeds are no more. They have become something else. The seeds are gone and have metamorphosed into a sprout. Then the sprout becomes the first leaves of the plant. The plant keeps changing and becoming something new.

We can continue the development of the sunflower in our imagination. We can follow it forward in time until the sunflower creates new seeds. We can also follow the sunflower backward in time and tuck the seeding plant back into the original seed from which it began. In this way we have reached into the past as well as perceived what is coming from the future. We can compare the differences in our life of feeling as we experience these two movements in time—-coming from the past and from the future.

GOLDEN GRAINS

Grains are very special seeds, indeed little golden gems, ripened in the abundance of light and warmth of several seasons. To really appreciate these little treasures we must take a walk in a field of waving young corn, barley, wheat, or oats. Many times during the summer I visit fields of barley and oats to witness the grains turning from green to yellow to golden as blue cornflowers come to bloom in between the stalks. A feeling of awe and admiration fills me as I observe the loveliness of the countryside enveloping the fields in the hot noon sun. It is such a glorious feeling that I clearly sense the fullness of the space and the activity surrounding the grains. In my imagination these activities that I perceive are nature beings whirling above the field, concentrating cosmic light and warmth, packing the starry world into each tiny kernel.

These fields of grains are like fields of sunbeams anchored strongly in the earth. I observe the uprightness of the sturdy stalks and how they unite directly, as in a straight line, with the center of the earth. I become aware of the small clusters of mature grains on top of each stalk, little golden crowns connected to the periphery of the cosmos. I feel my own uprightness grounded firmly in the earth as I strive to unite my thinking with cosmic thoughts.

As I taste the soft, milky, green juices of young spring wheat and later bite into the hardier mature wheat grain, I try to fathom what is happening within these golden treasures. The substances in these ripened grains—the minerals, starches, oils, and proteins—have become the carriers of new life. The processes that produced the minerals abundant in the roots, the starches in the leaves, and the oils in the flower and seed are all present in the mature grains. Together with the most recently fashioned proteins, they form an ideal balance for new life. These substances in the wheat kernels will, when planted in the soil, attract the creative forces outside of themselves. In the future when the wheat begins to sprout, the life forces will manifest once more, grow a new field of wheat and, following the reproduction of fresh new grains, withdraw again. Hidden within the sheath of each grain is an ordered little cosmos of its own, totally independent of its mother plant, capable of producing thousands of new grains in years to come! There is nothing like the wholeness of grains.

Traditionally grains came to humanity as gifts from the Divine. Legends from around the world have preserved this relationship between the people, the grains, and the spiritual world. In China the country folks asked their gods for a food they could eat every day, and they were given rice. The Greek goddess Demeter asked the farmers for barley in their worshipping of her. German priests celebrated the spring fertility rituals to the goddess Nertho with oats. Newlywed couples were showered with millet (shifting later to rice) as they asked for blessings from the goddess of love and fertility. The Upanishads relate the wholeness of grains to the Creator, and many Native American Indian stories describe how the Great Spirit asked the Corn Mother to give her life to the people of all nations to eliminate hunger forever.

When running my hands through the sacks of whole grains in my pantry, I feel these divine gifts bursting with potential. These golden grains, fruit and seed in all, came to life under the stars, moon, and sun and have breathed in the light forces longer than any other plant food we eat. I sense how the oats embrace these cosmic forces as if they had wrapped the future into the ripening seed. Rice grains hidden in Egyptian pyramids have successfully sprouted 4,000 years after they were placed there. Like a mother's gift of sweet, nourishing milk, cereal grains bring wholeness, vitality, and strength to humanity. They are golden treasures for all people of all nations.

LIVING INTO THE FLOWING ACTIVITY OF LIFE

We cook with many different vegetables, fruits, seeds, and grains, and may wonder which part of each plant we are working with. We can begin by laying them out on a table in a circle resembling the development of the archetypal plant: seeds on the far left and right, edible flowers in the upper middle, and roots on the lower part of the table. It is probably easy to place the carrots, pumpkin seeds, and leafy greens, but where does the onion go? Many vegetable plants have been cultivated to hold back a natural process or to swell certain parts. Could the onion be a swollen stalk? The green broccoli looks like a bouquet of little buds just days before they set flowers. The cauliflower is white and hard—is it a flower? The big, round, firm cabbage may be a bud or leafy greens held back from flowering. The snow peas in their pods seem to be more like fruits than fresh seeds. Scallions look like contracted slender leaves. But what about potatoes—are they roots or thickened stems? What parts of the plants are the watery cucumber and the peculiar little brussels sprouts growing on the stem at the foot of each leaf?

After laying all the vegetables on the table, compare the vegetables to each other and observe what forces and growth processes were most active in each one. The earthly forces are so dominant in the carrots, yet we can sense some flowery qualities in the orange color. When we compared the carrot to the burdock root we experience the much stronger earthly quality in the burdock.

When comparing the vegetables we can go a step deeper and inwardly open ourselves to the activities and processes that created the foods. Within inner silence, create a living, detailed image of leafy green kale. When you feel totally present to the growth processes of the leafy kale, feel the growing, spreading, drawing upwards and outward-reaching movement of the leaves. Like the leaves, sense a quiet conversation with cosmic warmth and light. Stay with this feeling a while.

In place of the leafy green kale, now create a living image of a parsnip and experience how these roots are of the cool, moist, dark soil. Feel how the parsnip is drawn down, ever deeper as it becomes sweeter, stronger, and heavier with matter.

When we live into these processes, the musicality, wisdom, and intensity of the gestures of each vegetable will be able to express themselves. We experience deeply the inner qualities of growth and maturing and sense what is coming to be. No longer will we just see a carrot or any other food as a mere object, but we will see and really feel the beauty of the wisdom within this food, how it came into being, and how we can continue the creative process in the kitchen. Seeing in this way is a living way of seeing; it is seeing with much more than what meets the eyes.

Every time we work in the kitchen we can encourage this way of seeing and observe a genuine feeling of reverence, wonder, and enthusiasm. We can create an imagination of the metamorphosing creative forces and experience a wisdom-filled world with all its rhythms and expanding and condensing forces. Soon we will begin to notice how these same forces are active within our own pots and pans. In later chapters we will discover how different cutting and cooking styles soften or harden, expand and contract, elevate or densify, and relax or strengthen the food as we prepare the different dishes. Cooking is essentially an ethereal process, a continuation of the creative processes in nature.

When we experience food and cooking in this manner we attend to the flowing activity of life itself. With practice we begin to sense these same forces within ourselves. Gradually we will develop a reverent feeling of being within what has not yet come into form, what is yet forming. Perhaps for a moment we will feel at one with these invisible active forces and the wisdom permeating this ever-changing world.

COLLECTING VEGETABLES

Selecting seasonal vegetables for our meal can be a rich and joyful experience independent of having a garden. Whether we collect our food from our backyard, at the local grocery, or gather wild foods in nature, we have an opportunity to fully relate to the foods we choose to cook with.

To care for vegetables and observe them grow is a very intimate experience. If a garden plot is not available, raising plants in a pot in a southern-facing window can create a similar deep experience. Herbs are especially well suited for this; basil, parsley, thyme, oregano, rosemary, chives, and sage are but a few.

Every time I plant a seed in the ground I am in awe of the archetypal cycle that I see in it—the metamorphoses from seed to leaf to bud, blossom, fruit, and seed. I am amazed that a sunflower seed blossoms within weeks into a sunflower, greeting the sun on its journey across the sky. Only a sunflower will grow from that seed, not a squash or anything else! What a miracle! My assistance in this process is humble. I nurture the plant with rich compost and make sure it has water. Then I watch the plant with the utmost interest and attention. I see the ethereal life forces that bring this plant into manifestation and I sense the nature beings busily working around and within it. When it is time to harvest, it is with the deepest respect and appreciation that I reach out in joy to pick the food.

In America an abundance of produce is available at all times. It is quite a different experience to collect our vegetables at the market rather than growing them ourselves, yet it can still be intimate. At the market the shelves and bins are already filled with a cornucopia of colors, forms, and shapes—a variety of vegetables and fruits, many from other parts of the world.

✤ Explore

Brainstorm all that is involved
in getting your meal together.
Write down everything that comes
to mind. Observe how the list
quickly becomes extremely long.

At the marketplace I imagine I am at an art gallery, looking at beautiful artwork created by an extraordinary artist. I admire each piece as it lies there with its friends in the bin. Who and what could create this exceptional, magnificent artwork? One at a time I hold different vegetables in my hand. I look at their shapes, their colors, smell them and feel their texture. I imagine how the mother plant of the vegetable looked in the field. I see how it grew from a tiny sprout to a full, mature plant. I follow the growth of the plant in relationship to the seasons and sense its connection to the warmth, air, water, and the soil.

While looking at the vegetable, I appreciate all the activities and people involved in getting the food into my grocery bag. I feel gratitude toward the rain, the bumble-bee, the farmer's hard work, the makers of the farm tools and machinery, the truck drivers, distributors, managers, and clerks at the store. It is quite astonishing what is involved in getting our food to our table.

We can create still another experience when we go foraging by a stream, a field, a park, or an edge of a forest to find fresh edible wild plants. In the city we might be concerned with pollution, but compared to the experience of picking our own fresh food it is not much to worry about.

The early spring is a great time to pick fresh, nourishing nettles. They are one of the first plants to peek out of the ground after the snow has disappeared. Their tender top shoots can be picked for food until the nettle begins to flower about one to two months later.

Spring is also a wonderful time to collect dandelion leaves and flowers, early clover blossoms, wild onions, chickweed, and over-wintered burdock roots. At the source of a stream we can find crisp watercress during spring, fall, and winter. The summer and fall are the time to gather a variety of berries, wild apples, plums, and cherries, as well as dig for dandelion, horseradish, and other wild roots.

If we go to the same place often, we will be able to follow a plant's development from the first early leaves to the mature fruit that seeds in the fall. Sometimes we can bring a magnifying glass to help us stay present to the wonders we encounter. One way to increase our attentiveness and sharpen our perception is to draw the plant, for example the stinging nettle, in its different developmental stages. When we draw something we really observe what is in front of us. I draw only what I see unfold before my eyes, as realistically as possible. After that I close my eyes and "draw" the nettle in all details in my imagination. Then I erase the image and sit quietly with the life-filled space left in place of the plant. After a while I observe if there is an after-image that lingers with me.

When it is time for me to pick the plant for food, I sit down with appreciation in my heart. I take a seat among the leaves and grasses, listen to the birds, smell the fragrances, and sense the moisture of the earth. There seems to be a friendliness and business of the place totally of its own. It feels like industrious nature beings are working deliberately and intentionally all around me. It is as if the beauty and gentleness of the place bring them to life in me. When I leave with a handful of food for my dinner, I feel the gratitude that wells up within from a fountain of joy. Life is abundant! Life is beautiful!

THE WATER OF LIFE

 Explore

Cut an onion in half from top to bottom. Can you see a rhythmical pattern similar to what you see in a flowing stream?

Does this cut onion look like the arrested movement of water? Look around in nature for other "snapshots" of movement expressed as form.

When we sit beside a flowing stream watching the moving water, we have with certainty a feeling of the liveliness and transitory nature of the solid and earthly. Water is so different from the firmness of the unyielding ground. It is unformed, open, flexible, and perceptible to everything in its surrounding. First we notice the cold water bursting forth from every crack in the hillside. It seems like water always wishes to travel and change. It never wants to be still. It constantly seeks to sink low or else to rise up high as steam. Around the watercress and other plants that grow at the mouth of the stream we become aware of small waves on the surface that are apparently staying the same. Underneath the surface the water is moving and never the same, but on the surface the waves look like they are at rest. In amazement we realize that water creates patterns. Whenever it is in movement it has a natural capacity to create beautiful, rhythmical flow patterns.[4] It makes us wonder who and what creates these incredibly beautiful patterns. What interplay between what forces is taking place?

Water is the basis of all life-sustaining processes. Water makes life possible! How fascinating it is to observe the first new onion shoots in spring being lifted into the warm air from the moist, saturated, soft earth. We notice that these first young plants actually look fluid themselves. Have the same forces we discovered in the moving stream entered into these budding stages of new growth? It appears

---

[4] *Sensitive Chaos* by Theodor Schwenk.

that the creative life forces actually penetrate our material world through water, and that water itself is the mediator of the invisible, spiritual world. We come to realize that form comes about through movement of fluids—fluids penetrated by creative life forces. Form is slowed-down movement! Our sprouting onion is a glimpse of movement in time!

The sphere of our planet is enveloped in and saturated with water. Water circulates as the heart-blood of the earth. It penetrates every living organism. Water lives. It flows down to lake and ocean, rises and travels in the air, gathers as clouds, falls to the ground as rain or snow, before it hurries down into the streams and the rivers, back again to the lakes and oceans.

The fields and gardens are part of this great circulation. When we look at our sprouting onion in the wet, saturated, warm spring soil we notice that it is also enveloped in water. The water contained in the mists around the plant and in the earth surrounding the roots steps selflessly into the growing onion sprout. Here it unifies with the cosmic and earthly forces where it pulsates ever so gently with the rhythms of the moon, earth, and cosmos.

When it is time to cook the onion, the water or juice of the onion meets the water in the soup pot. There the liquids become the midwife in birthing new tastes and textures as well as enriching and enhancing unique qualities in the meal. After we ingest the soup, the liquids once more serve as mediator, this time within the human being. Here it makes chemical interactions possible and pulsates rhythmically and harmoniously with the remarkable individual processes of digestion and creation.

MESSAGES FROM WATER

The flexibility and receptivity of life-sustaining water is so fascinating that many pioneering researchers have investigated the differences in the quality and vitality of water from various sources. One scientist from California, Masaru Emoto, began to photograph water crystals made from samples he had gathered in the environment. His book[5] contains hundreds of photographs of ice crystals, each completely different from the others. Wherever the water came from unpolluted, natural sources, beautiful and complete ice crystals formed. The crystals appeared quite the opposite when made from contaminated and heavily treated water.

---

[5] *Messages from Water* by Masaru Emoto.

Other contemporary researchers, using different processes, have also documented the change of quality in the water taken from vegetables grown in different environments. They even looked at changes made by various cooking methods. Their scientific methods and pictures[6] revealed how life forces in the fluids changed according to how various foods were grown and cooked. High-quality foods expressed delicate rhythmical patterns of vortices radiating in all directions around a center. Poorer quality water or overcooked foods showed imbalanced and uneven forms.

Masaru Emoto raised the question, "If water is so receptive to these very subtle outer influences, could water then be responsive to thinking as well?" He continued his experiments and documented how water responded to the music, thoughts, emotions, and words it was exposed to. Different exposures produced either lovely, sublime crystals or mundane, ugly crystals. He concluded that water is definitely influenced by how it is treated. It is not only physical pollution that contaminates the water; what we think and feel when around water also fundamentally changes the quality of it. This confirms what we perhaps always have intuitively known: the importance of a healthy inner life of the cook for the well-being of the family, humanity, and the entire earth. In Denmark an old saying suggests that when a meal is well prepared, tastes delicious, and is digested well, "the cook sang over the pots." The melodies we perceive in our hearts surely contribute to the wholeness of the meal.

COOKING WATER

Creation mythologies from around the world bring us pictures of the primeval water, the primordial womb of life, from which all emerged. The Great Mother of All, the cosmic warmth and light, manifested in the flowing, ever-moving, unformed abyss of water. From this life-permeated water arose all existence. Worldwide cultures recognized water to be imbued with life and the carrier of the creative life forces. Up until the beginning of our technical age, people perceived in wonder living nature beings or water nymphs in every spring and river, lake and well. Every body of water was infused with life unique to its environment.

Similar living pictures well up within me as I fill my soup pot with water from the kitchen faucet. In my imagination I see the water coming from a dark, underground cave enclosed by majestic rocks, overflowing with fresh, crystal clear water. Like liquid gold held in the hands of the goddesses, this precious water flows right

Explore

Compare how you feel after having eaten meals cooked with negative emotions and frustration versus meals cooked with gratitude and enthusiasm. These are very subtle observations that do not need to grow into judgments.

---

[6] The copper chloride crystallization method and round filter chromatography were developed by Ehrenfried Pfeiffer.

into my pot. How wonderful it tastes, so cool and refreshing.

Some people choose to use bottled water for cooking instead of city water or filtered water. Bottled water may be clean and contain only the natural elements that it had when it left the ground. However, when water is confined it remains still—there is no movement and little life. Such water loses its life force and vitality. Modern spiritual scientists have invented a way to recharge water with life forces through rhythmical movements using flow forms.[7] By running water through these flow forms it is refreshed and becomes vibrant and full of life again. I have not yet cooked with water that has been revived through flow forms, but I can imagine in the future it may be a possible way to revitalize the bottled water so popular today. No matter where our water comes from, whether it arrives from an underground well, a spring, bottle, or city plant, it is precious, life-giving water with individual character receptive to divine forces. Water is the foundation of all life.

TREASURES FROM THE PULSING SEA

 Explore

Most of the earth's surface is bathed in salty, mineral-rich ocean water. The coastline where sunlight is able to penetrate the water provides the richest area for plant growth in temperate climates. There the "grasses of the sea," also called sea vegetables, grow in abundance. These plants are ancient and relatively simple. They produce no seeds, fruits, or flowers. Their fronds are undifferentiated plants, held and supported by the buoyancy of the ocean water. On land the buoyancy of invisible cosmic forces, which create the upward-striving and outspreading gestures of each plant, undeniably hold the land vegetables upright. Sea vegetables, by contrast, are more influenced by the forces of the earth than is the plant growing in the field. They collapse without the buoyancy and support of the life-sustaining ocean water.

Buy a package of wakame or alaria sea vegetable. Soak some of it in a bowl of water. After a few minutes unfold the fronds and observe how the plant moves beautifully and gracefully with the water. Notice how the plant collapses when you pull it out of the water.

The constantly changing, moving ocean and the rhythmical daily rise and fall of the sea level dominate the life of all ocean plants. They live in and as the pulsing rhythm of the mineral-rich water. Wave after wave, tide after tide toss these ocean plants to and fro. In this demanding environment these sea vegetables develop tremendous strength, flexibility, persistence, and adaptability. No wonder many cultures included small amounts of sea vegetables in their diet to gain these qualities themselves.

Most sea vegetables live attached and anchored to solid rocks. Sea vegetables

---

[7] *Flowforms: The Rhythmic Power of Water* by John Wilkes.

are not the easiest to harvest. They grow in wet, slippery places. The fronds have to be foraged when the tide is low, often on a cold spring or autumn morning. When my husband and I lived in the northern part of Norway, we had the most incredible experiences harvesting sea vegetables. Dressed very warm in waders, we walked out into the receding tide and reverently collected these small ocean treasures. As crabs scurried to find a hiding place for a few hours during ebb tide, we reached out to cut the sea vegetables from the rocks. Standing with these ocean plants in our hands we could feel the powers of the majestic ocean. Strongly influenced by the moon, the ocean seemed to have concentrated its life forces into these little simple plants. Almost all minerals and fibers, they were so powerfully attached to their environment it was impossible to separate them from the rocks without a sharp knife. Right there we understood the reasons the northern coastal societies valued this hardy, strengthening food so much.

Sea salt is another treasure harvested naturally from the mighty ocean. We may not think of sea salt as a food, but actually it is a very precious ingredient in today's cooking. It is remarkable that only sun-drying creates real natural sea salt with its abundance of rich minerals and trace elements. Although trace minerals are very minute, they have great importance in our diets.

Ocean water is saturated with cosmic forces, activities, and rhythms. As sea salt is dried by the sun, it condenses the essences and processes from the life-permeated sea into the substance we know as sea salt. Natural sea salt is a hardened, solidified, crystallized substance. Redissolve the sea salt in water and observe that the physical, solid shapes of this substance completely disappear. They are no longer visible or tangible. The sea salt has selflessly given itself to the water and permeated it through and through. The condensed mineral processes have become available and active again in water. Naturally dried sea salt, referred to by early alchemists as "the flowers of the waves," is a treasure containing hidden powers of cosmic origin.

CELEBRATING THE
SEASONAL FESTIVALS

Indigenous cultures around the world celebrated the spring and fall equinoxes and the summer and winter solstices. When the traditional religions began, their festivals were also celebrated around the solstices and equinoxes. Over time the religions gradually removed the experiences of the seasons from their festival celebrations. They no longer have any significant connection to nature and the rhythmical interweaving of cosmic and earthly forces. As religious practices separated from the yearly cycles, so did humanity slowly separate from the living world with which it is so interconnected.

Today there is a resurgence of interest in a renewal of the festivals. Many sense a longing to reunite with the living world in a practical way. We know in our hearts that the spiritual essence is active in the life processes taking place within the seasons. Intuitively we feel that nature holds the key to the festivals and that our spiritual practices should not become separated from life as it breathes through the year.

The way to renew these traditional festivals is to re-create a genuine interest in nature and to contemplate the true meaning of each of the festivals we celebrate and its place in the life cycle of the earth. Only then will we have a living experience of the divine spirit as it weaves throughout the seasonal and hemispheric changes.

We can be more observant of our connection with the divine spirit and how it interweaves in our daily lives by bringing attention to the times of transformation from day into night, night into day, and the yearly seasons. These significant times offer unique opportunities to unite with the divine forces radiating powerfully in the world. When we deeply experience inwardly the spring and summer growth and the declining of fall and winter, we enter into the divine will of the world in the

❀ *Explore*

Keep a journal during the
yearly festivals that you celebrate.
Write down what lives in your
thinking, what feeling emerges,
and what you are motivated
and inspired to do. How do you
experience the differences in your
inner life during the summer and
winter months, spring and fall?

What is the significance of
each of the festivals and why
do you celebrate them?

widest possible way. Our experience of the living world becomes real and genuine as we become conscious of the breathing rhythms in nature and begin to sense these outer changes in our own inner soul life. The moods of the seasons, the moon phases, planetary movements, and the different parts of the days are within us and fashion our soul and body.

We are familiar with the feeling of the dark, cold, cozy winter days and how different this feeling is from the light, warm, dreamy mood of summer. Many also sense the difference between the full moon and the new moon. Nearly everyone notices the variations in the course of the day. The morning brings a completely different inner mood and bodily experience than the evening.

Poetically, I imagine and sense the life forces of the earth as a radiant cloak of divine light belonging to the spirit of the earth, the Spirit of Love, whom to me is Christ. As the radiant cloak draws in during the wintertime, I imagine the interior of the earth, the womb, shining deeper and brighter as the earth continues her inbreath. From a cosmic perspective I envision the earth being a brilliant golden star. Inwardly I am connected with this divine light and let it glow within me.

In spring I feel the divine light being exhaled with the life forces of the earth as the world manifests abundance of new life. I imagine the radiant cloak of light expanding into the cosmos. I unite myself with this jubilation; my inner soul life becomes one with the greening world.

I picture the forces at summer solstice, the height of this out breath, meeting and interweaving with the cosmic forces streaming toward the earth. I sense a kind of dialog or conversation taking place. In this conversation I picture an exchange of visions and questions of destiny. I imagine my own soul/spirit-light echoing this cosmic dialog. I weave a basket in my heart to catch the fruits coming from the spiritual world. Enthusiasm, joy, and anticipation of what is to come permeate my being.

When the radiant cloak of light in late summer and early fall begins to draw back toward the earth again, I imagine the visions and renewed forces from the summer's dialog interweaving with the light. I sense my inner strength emerge with the courage to be true to my own destiny. I feel the spirit-light brightening within me as it joins with the world community of divine light.

I see this archetypal drama moving rhythmically in waves throughout the planet earth, changing seasonally with the hemispheric breathing. I imagine humanity uniting itself with these hemispheric breathing forces and, in doing so, the divine light becoming stronger and brighter as the earth, a star, grows brighter and more spiritual.

COOKING, AN ESSENTIAL ASPECT OF A SPIRITUAL PATH

When we connect ourselves with the rhythmical breathing of the divine light, we express it through the art of cooking. Cooking, an everyday activity for everyone, articulates our spiritual connection to life more than anything else. Through the living art of cooking we unite with the spiritual essence breathing within the seasons and the food it produces. In the kitchen we consciously balance and complement the natural breathing of the year and the seasonal foods though various cooking styles.

In the summer heat, when the cosmic expansive forces are most active, we include cooling leafy salads with our meals, and in the cold winter we create warming stews with many grounding, earthy root vegetables. This is cooking and eating in harmony with the seasonal breathing. The art of cooking elevates these activities and gives us a feeling that what we do in the kitchen is an offering, a holy action done for the love of the world. This is an essential aspect of any spiritual path that anyone is invited to embark on.

In addition, we can appreciate how natural wholesome foods support the clarity of mind and peaceful feelings that we want to create, especially around the festivals. At the time of the solstices and the equinoxes, windows open wider to the spiritual world. I feel that the veil between the physical and the spiritual world is thinner. I want to celebrate these moments and not weigh myself down or set myself on an emotional roller coaster by indulging in fatty, rich meals accompanied by wine and overly sweet deserts. These are sacred times when I share my intentions, gratitude, questions, and experiences, and listen in a deeper way to the great secrets of life and divine guidance.

A GIFT FOR NATURE

One other way I have enlivened my relationship to the seasonal festivals and the processes in nature has been to spray my land and garden with biodynamic preparations. Biodynamic preparations are made of substances from the farm, prepared in harmony with the seasonal rhythms and the natural processes of the earth and cosmos. I think of them as homeopathic remedies for the garden or the land. Some preparations I make myself and other preparations I get from our local group of biodynamic farmers. Only a very small amount is used in gallons of clear, fresh rainwater. The preparations are stirred for 20 minutes to one hour before they are sprayed on the land, some in the evening and some in the morning.

 Explore

Fill a big bucket halfway with rainwater. Use your hand to create vortexes first one way, then the other. Feel gratitude for the source of life as you stir. Then walk around, in your garden or in your neighborhood, spreading the water potentized with these thoughts and feelings.

At each of the four main seasonal festivals, celebrated around the solstices and equinoxes, I gather a variety of appropriate preparations and mix them with water. I sit in an inner mood of joy and gratitude while stirring the water rhythmically. If I do not have the right preparations, I sit and stir a gallon of rainwater for half an hour, adding only the reverence and appreciation. I use my hand to make a vortex going in the direction of the sun (clockwise). Then I create chaos with my hand by stirring the opposite way, creating a vortex going against the direction of the sun (counterclockwise). I continue stirring in this manner until it is ready to spray.

In one hand I carry this potent water in a small bucket. In the other hand I carry a little dust-brush. Then I dip a small dust-brush in the water and spray it every 20 to 30 steps on our land and garden. As I spray I attend to the gratitude in my heart. I walk around in this mood through the woods, garden, and in the fields. This is my gift to the earth!

A LIVING RELATIONSHIP WITH THE LAND

Cultures of the past were aware that their crops received nourishment from the earth as well as from the ordered rhythm of life—the universe, the sun, and the stars. They worked the land according to their observations and they treated their animals, plants, grains, and soil in a way that reflected this relationship. Biodynamic gardeners and farmers of today keep building on this respectful relationship.

Biodynamic farmers experience their farms as individual, self-sustaining, living organisms that live and breathe with the earth in a sea of cosmic life forces. Everything is alive for the biodynamic farmer or gardener and maintains connection to the spiritual cosmic world. The farmer or gardener sees it as his or her duty to act as a steward to maintain and foster this connection. S/he prepares the soil in such a way that it enables plants to take up the cosmic influences necessary for their growth, by using special biodynamic preparations.

Scientist, artist, and philosopher Rudolf Steiner inspired these biodynamic preparations, which are made and used with the understanding of how the earthly and cosmic forces interplay throughout the year. He introduced a new way of thinking about the relationship of the soil to the forces of the cosmos. Steiner recognized that plants grow with the support of the cosmic forces. These forces and activities stream into the earth through the living nature of the soil and its minerals. The quality and life forces of the food we eat influence the quality of our thinking, feeling, and interaction with people and nature. In turn, our thinking, feeling, and way of interacting create the future condition of our society and the world. Steiner felt that a renewal of agriculture was necessary to reestablish the relationship between the cosmos and humanity, for the world. He introduced the biodynamic preparations in order to re-enliven the earth so that the starry world, the cosmic forces and activities, again could find their way to the soil and our food.

What distinguishes biodynamic farming from other healthy farming practices such as permaculture and organic farming is that biodynamic farmers consciously think and work in a practical way with these earthly and cosmic substances, forces, and activities. Sowing and harvesting are carefully done at the most favorable times in relationship to the sun, moon cycles, and planetary rhythms. In addition to applying biodynamic preparations and composted manure, these farmers also maintain healthy soil by practicing crop rotations, incorporating plenty of organic matter, and other holistic practices.

Animals, especially cows, also play a big part in the life of the biodynamic farm and ensure a cycling of substances and life forces. Cows are grazers and have an elaborate digestive system. They eat grasses and other roughage and in return produce rich manure permeated with their own life forces and qualities. When the soil receives this valuable cow manure, composted with biodynamic preparations, its soil life is enhanced. This composted manure creates nourishing humus that is able to draw in the beneficial forces of the sun, moon, stars, and planets, which in turn supports healthy plants.

Ideally, every biodynamic farm or garden has its own beehives as well. Bees live entirely in the world of air, light, and warmth and are an essential part of the interrelationship of the cosmic forces.

In many areas of the world, scientific research is carried out to develop a better understanding of the quality of biodynamic foods and farming practices. Ideas are implemented, observations made, comparative testing done, and elaborate evaluation made in search for quality food and life for everybody in a living world filled with spirit.

COOKING AS A LIVING ART

In my experience, cooking is one of the finest and most important arts given to humanity. Through the art of cooking we sustain the activity of life—body, soul, and spirit—to enable us to fulfill our life's purpose and destiny. Nothing less!

The cook as artist sees how the activities in the kitchen flow together with the processes of the living world. In the kitchen we begin to cook with the ripe, so-called end manifestation of cosmic and earthly forces—the roots, leaves, fruits, and seeds. We take these foods and, through cooking, further enliven, enrich, and transform them. With a deeper understanding for what is in progress and what wants to be expressed, we create healthy seasonable meals. We make dishes that embrace the dynamic of change, balancing the individual changing conditions and the changes in our environment. Cooking is surely a living art closely linked to the health of humanity.

The painter's workplace is his or her art studio. The cook's art studio is the kitchen. Before either of them begins to create, they get their workplace in order. The painter gets the canvas stretched, gets the different brushes ready, and chooses the colors s/he wants to work with. Likewise the cook brings out cutting board, pots and pans, sharpened knives, and utensils, and chooses colorful ingredients for his or her creations. Before starting, both might have an idea of what they want to create. The painter might want to paint the mood of the moonlit seashore with gusty winds. The cook wants to make a meal that balances the cool weather of the day, the season of the year, and may decide on a warming, nourishing colorful stew and freshly baked muffins with side dishes of stir-fried leafy greens and pickled beets.

Most importantly, as the painter paints, s/he lives into the moonlit seashore with his or her whole being. Similarly the cooking artist goes beyond theories, recipes, and techniques and lives into the activity of life itself. The cook penetrates the heart

 Explore

What is the mood of your art studio, your kitchen? How does it feel? How would you like it to be?

of truth from which all life originates and imbues his or her cooking with a liveliness and freshness that reflects this truth.

The painter will study color theories, art history, the warmth and coolness of the colors, perspective, lines, strokes, and much more. The cook who approaches cooking as an art will also study and bring knowledge together with common sense, imagination, and intuition in free exploration. S/he will observe the secrets of nature and how and where the ingredients s/he wants to use originate. The cook would want to know what brought them into being and what forces and processes were active in the creation of theses foods. S/he will want to learn about different cutting techniques and cooking methods, understand the effects of cooling and warming food and dishes, and discover how to enhance different qualities, tastes, and textures. Perhaps s/he is interested in learning about traditional and historical uses of foods or cooking styles and herb lore from the region s/he lives in. S/he might also want to learn about how to cook for different health conditions and temperaments and how to cook to support what s/he wants to become in life.

One of the most interesting things I learned as a painter was to understand how the magnificent colors are created from the interplay of light and darkness. At night I watched the sky, pitch black with sparkles of stars shimmering in the distance. In the day I looked at the same dark sky through the light of the sun and what I saw was blue! In the evening I looked at the sunset, the concentrated light through layers of darkening atmosphere. The light intensified from bright yellow to orange and red as the sun got closer to the horizon and more layers of atmosphere, of darkness, came between the light and me as the observer. Right then I understood that all the magnificent, qualitatively different colors I saw were created from the interplay of the light and darkness.[8]

It is very similar with cooking. We as cooks continue to work with ethereal cosmic and earthly forces (the light and darkness) to make a multitude of magnificent, colorful, and qualitatively different dishes and meals.

Because we can continue in the kitchen the creative process that nature began, we can enjoy and digest a variety of wonderful foods and dishes, which would otherwise not be accessible to us. We can completely transform the foods that we work with. The art of cooking teaches us, for example, how to change raw indigestible grains into wholesome breads, muffins, cakes, delicious pancakes, waffles, porridges, noodles, spaghetti, and more. By preparing food in different ways, different qualities

---

[8] *Color Theory*, Johann von Wolfgang Goethe.

in the food come about. We can use various cutting styles and cooking methods to change the nutritional elements of the dishes and create a variety of tastes, fragrances, and textures. Visually, qualitatively, and nutritiously, the cooking artist can create a meal beautifully balanced between lightness and darkness. This is truly a living art.

Every day, right in the kitchen, we have an opportunity to approach our daily cooking artistically in an attitude of awe and reverence. How enriching and empowering to consciously co-create with nature in the kitchen!

ENTERING THE KITCHEN

I enter my kitchen with deep silence. It is not a silence that is void of outer noise, but an inner silence and calmness centered in the heart. This silence makes everything a whole and holy oneness pregnant with potentials.

As I begin to cook I am warmed by quiet enthusiasm. Reverence and wonder fill my heart as I look at each of the ingredients I choose to work with. I see the creations of nature: her beauty, colors, and expressions. Gratitude wells up as I think of the bounty she provides to humanity, endlessly producing, endlessly giving, selflessly.

This inner silence prepares me for being fully attentive and present to creative inspiration. Cooking is a process of listening and co-creating.

If I feel tired, irritated, or in a rush, I either take some time for myself to reconnect, pull something out of the freezer, or make quick sandwiches. I know too well that cooking with these emotions is not wise. If I cook when I feel distracted or exhausted I add those feelings to the dish. When I feel a lack of focus or the presence of negativity, I also close off any creative imagination, inspiration, or intuition as I work. Those are the days where I use too much fire, burn food in the pot, and overcook the soup. Cooking then feels more like a chore that I need to hurry and get done with.

A friend of mine told me that when she was young and living in India with her family and grandparents, her grandmother would sit down to cook. She had a small, clearly marked area as her kitchen and a stove made of clay to work on. It was a sacred place where no one was to enter except her. She kept it clean and painted the stovetop every other day. Before she began to cook, she took a bath and cleared her thoughts and emotions. In many cultures the activity of cooking used to take place in a special revered space and cooking itself was regarded as a sacred act.

 Explore

How do you most often enter your kitchen? Are you tired? Is preparing meals a chore?

Do you wash your hands attentively and clear your mind before cooking?

Do you want to make any changes in how you prepare yourself before you begin to cook?

ATTENDING TO ATTENTIVENESS

Working in the kitchen gives us an opportunity to deepen our relationship with the world through the food we cook. We can look at the ingredients as if we are seeing them for the first time and attend to them as we would with close friends. When we create genuine interest for what we are working with, we engage our senses. It is through the senses that the wisdom of the world conveys its nature to us.

We are accustomed to thinking we have five senses: seeing, hearing, smelling, tasting, and touching. In reality we have seven more: the sense of balance, movement, speech, and thought as well as the sense of self, life, and warmth.[9] Notice that when we work in the kitchen we constantly apply and exercise our inner sense of balance. We relate this sense of balance to cutting styles, cooking styles, colors, and so forth. As we move our hands over the surfaces of the vegetables, we feel a sense of movement and how our own inner movement relates and resonates harmoniously with the movements and processes that created the foods we are preparing. All kinds of curves, textures, and contours are expressed to us. We perceive the unique yet universal language articulated by the foods and dishes we cook.

Our sense of thought also engages during cooking. By immersing ourselves in the creative processes our thinking becomes like the life forces we work with: mobile and living. We clearly have a sense of life. Not only do we sense our own well-being, whether we are tired or comfortable, we also sense the life of the food we cook. We have an inner sense of warmth when we eat spicy foods or a hot soup, and we feel warmth by sharing our meal with friends and family. Lastly we have a sense of self, of our spirit-nature and the spirit-nature of others. We nurture this sense through the fact that we are able to imbue and change the quality of foods with our own activity. When we bring consciousness in our senses, cooking becomes an enriching, living, soul/spirit experience of the living world.

Attentive and open in all senses, begin to look with curiosity at the foods needed for the meal. Observe the structures, the rhythms, and follow the patterns into the slightest details. Keep your eyes on the ingredients as if you were touching them with your gaze. Run your eyes up and down, around and inside. What are the movements and gestures of these foods and what secrets do they tell? Without intellectual speculation, look through a magnifying glass and admire the work of nature. What beauty to behold!

Try to really live into the processes that created the vegetables. Immerse deeply

Explore

Cut an apple horizontally, right through the middle where it is broadest. You will discover a beautiful five-pointed star. Nature is full of these awe-inspiring surprises.

---

[9] *Our Twelve Senses* by Albert Soesman.

in these activities of growth and decay, expanding and contracting. While washing the beet, become the beet as it grew in the dark moist soil. Rinse the kale and feel the upward and outward movement of these leafy greens. If the leaves are still attached to the stalk, observe the special ordered arrangement of the leaves to the stem, how they unfurl into planes, spiraling, stretching outward. Give yourself into the feeling that arises in you.

When we have these lovely colorful foods in front of us, we can look at them in such a way that we perceive what the spirit that lives throughout space expresses. At that moment we may feel that we are looking into the soul of the earth.

As we take a couple of onions in our hands, we admire the roundness and firmness of these vegetables. We observe how the outer layer is tightly protecting the bulb. Now cut the onion vertically from top to bottom. Notice how the creative formative force has shaped this onion and created the most beautiful patterns. Within the outer brown coat are layer after layer of what would become the new leaves next year if the onion were to be planted. These layers develop out of a base, which holds the new flowering shoot. If we look closely around this base we might find a separate new bulb growing, which would become the flowering onion the following year. How amazing to be able to witness something that will manifest in the future.

Uncooked as well as cooked vegetables and herbs have delicate fragrances. Breathe in the gentle scents of each of the foods before they are cooked. The delicate scent of these raw vegetables is an echo of the fragrance of the universe. Notice how all these fragrances change as the foods are cooked.

While cooking, watch also how the colors and the textures of the foods transform. Observe how the green string beans brighten and soften as they cook before they get to a point where they become pale with no luster, and mushy. The same happens when we boil kale; the color first deepens to a lovely, rich, dark green and then becomes dull when cooked for a longer time. Red radishes lose their color completely when cooked, while the bright orange color of hard winter squash intensifies in the cooking process, resembling concentrated sunlight.

What happens when we add salt to a dish? It makes a big difference whether salt is added in the beginning of the cooking time or at the end. Natural sea salt is permeated with strong contracting forces. Soak dried beans in salt water and you will find that they struggle to expand. Add sea salt when you start the cooking of the chickpeas and discover how difficult it is for them to get soft and tender. Notice how salt in small amounts can bring out the special flavors of each food and how some foods become sweeter when a pinch of sea salt is added.

Explore

Do you know when the food is done cooking just by listening to the sounds or smelling the aromas rising from the pots?

Feel the roughness of the leaves and the smoothness of the squash. Close your eyes and touch each food gently. Let your hands run through the salt crystals. Touch the cool, juicy part of the cucumber and become aware of the tiny seeds. Feel the layers of the cabbage and the rings of the onion. Notice how this light touch makes you aware of the borders of your own hands.

We might have a favorite dish that we like because it tastes delicious or looks fabulous. We may like a special dish because it is fun to cook or eat. Have you ever paid attention to which dish you like according to its sound? Listen! What does it sound like when we cut, simmer, or sizzle the foods for that dish? Notice the different sounds in our kitchen. Listen to the footsteps, the stirring of the pot, water splashing, and a lid placed on a pan. Are there any technical noises such as a heater, refrigerator, or fan?

Observe if the water, when it runs out of the kitchen sink, creates a vortex spiraling either clockwise or counterclockwise. Draw a spoon through a thick soup, first slowly, then a little faster. What patterns emerge? Observe the movements and shapes that appear while mixing dough and stirring sauces, or when the heat underneath the cooking pot sets the water in motion. When we sharpen our knives, wash the carrots, cut the cabbages, and wash the dishes, do we work harmoniously and rhythmically? Feel the loveliness of your own flowing, graceful movements.

Continue to stay attentive to all the changes and transformations that happen in your art studio, your kitchen. As the painter, take a few steps back to keep everything in perspective and observe your artwork, as it is being created, from a distance.

COOKING WITH NATURE

We can approach the year as an archetypal imagination of becoming: each season moving to the next and returning to where it started. Cooking with nature and her rhythms invites a spiraling cyclic path and the possibility to meet each time of year again and again in a new way. It encourages an inner development of mobility and flexibility and deepens our understanding and experiences year after year. We are given an opportunity to grow and learn, and the freedom to support health and harmony in the world. It is awesome and it is a great responsibility.

During my first macrobiotic cooking classes that I attended in the late 1970s, I gradually came to realize that individual health and peace in the world are closely connected to our relationship with food—how we perceive food, what we choose to eat, and how we prepare it. I understood that there is no "good" or "bad" food, and no one diet right for everybody. I became aware that foods are the revelation of spiritual presences, imbued with different properties. I understood that the food choices we make create various effects socially and economically.

My cooking instructors encouraged me to experiment and observe for myself so that I would rely on my own knowing. I began to notice that when I ate sugar I felt

Explore

Select two foods you frequently include in your diet and research their historical and traditional uses as well as the impact your choices have on the environment, individual health, health of humanity, and economy.

scattered, fragmented, and confused. It gave me an artificial high that later depleted me. I researched the history of sugar and traced its production in America back to the slave plantations in the South. I understood how it had influenced the economy and social life of many through the ages. I found that the introduction of sugar into the indigenous people's diets was detrimental to their health.[10] I could see no reason to support the sugar industry or include it in my diet, which made it very easy to eliminate.

I continued to experiment with various other foods. I researched their historical and traditional uses and understood the effects they had on society and the environment as well as on my thinking, emotions, activity, and stamina. Through my observations I realized that I used certain foods as a substitute for the inner work I needed to do myself. I became aware of how quantity changed quality, and comprehended deeply what moderation meant. I felt freedom entering my own decisions, along with a commitment to learn and understand as I continued to be my own researcher. I felt exhilarated knowing that I can take responsibility for my choices, not in a judgmental way but in an empowering way. I can do my best to cook and live in harmony with the earth and the cosmic rhythms. I can strive to create a right relationship with food, the environment, others, and myself for the love of world.

Through my many years of experience I have found that meals that nourish health and harmony in the world are created primarily of local and seasonal foods. Local seasonal foods resonate with the rhythmical changes of the environment we live in. They encourage a healthy relationship with nature and life itself. This is traditionally what people all over the world have practiced. It is only recently that we have been able to ship foods around the world.

I have also found that it is important to create a dynamic balance between the varieties of life forces and processes involved in the creation of the foods. When we use roots like carrots in our meal, we choose to eat a food that has been created within the cool dark soil and has been influenced primarily by grounding, mineralizing, earthly forces. When we use the carrot tops, we use a food that has been created through the rhythmical breathing of expansive and contractive forces and is more connected to the cosmic forces or forces of levity than the root is.

We are accustomed to thinking of the different substances found in our foods, such as minerals, fats, proteins, and carbohydrates, as being a "thing," fixed and unchangeable, but in reality all kinds of lively processes interact within these

---

[10] *Nutrition and Physical Degeneration* by Weston Price.

substances. These processes and activities are ingested with the food; however, they are immediately transformed and affect us in various ways. Most of us have had the experience of protein-rich foods affecting us differently than food abundant in carbohydrates. We have experienced that within the world of protein-rich foods, animal protein is a completely different quality than vegetable protein. Likewise we may sense that animal fats are of different quality and stimulate different processes within us than vegetable oils. We are also familiar with the various types and sources of carbohydrates—honey bringing different qualities than whole grains, for example. Similarly, within the world of minerals, we might know that calcium-rich foods create effects unlike those of magnesium-rich foods.

The way the food is prepared is equally or perhaps more important than selecting local, seasonal foods, understanding the life forces and processes that brought them into being, and the substances of each food. When we prepare foods using different cooking methods and cutting styles, we bring out different qualities in the dish. We change form, shapes, and colors of the foods and transform the nutritional elements and value of the dishes. We create a variety of tastes, fragrances, and textures, and we make the food we eat attractive and digestible. Take, for example, an onion: Eaten raw it is crisp, pungent, and has a cooling nature, whereas stewed it is sweet, soft, and warming.

 Explore

Take a look at yesterday's meals. Write down all the foods you ate. Which foods were grown locally and which were imported from other areas and other climates?

CUTTING STYLES—THE HARMONY OF FORM

Just as I select quality bristle brushes, paints, and paper when I paint, I select quality tools for cutting and cooking. My favorite vegetable knife is a very sharp, Oriental knife with a rectangular carbon steel blade. It lends itself to cut any vegetable in beautiful shapes and forms. There is no comparison to this knife, in my opinion. It is easy to manage and can be sharpened paper thin for various fine cuts.

I clean root vegetables with a simple natural vegetable brush, while I take great care to leave the skin undamaged. I rinse leafy greens and round vegetables well before I use them and make sure no dirt remains. I try to cut as little off the vegetables as possible and waste nothing. I use healthy trimmings for soup stocks or decorations.

I use natural wooden cutting boards. I keep a separate cutting board and knife for fish and animal foods. After cutting each vegetable, I clean the board and the knife with water. I use firm yet gentle rhythmical movements while cutting. The fingers on my left hand are slightly curled back as I hold the vegetables securely but

Explore

Do you feel different after eating root vegetables or fruits?

Cut up a couple of carrots and cook them in a little water for 10-15 minutes. Then cut similar size pieces of apples and cook them the same way. Eat one dish several hours after the other. Try the experiment over a couple of days.

All foods affect us differently. Did you notice any change in your thinking, emotions or physical being?

gently when I cut. I keep the cut vegetables separated on plates until all foods are sliced for the dish I am about to prepare.

The way the vegetables are cut is very important. It makes a real difference in how the finished dish will present itself, according to beauty, taste, texture, and what qualities are brought about in the food from the cutting style.

To illustrate this, peel an onion by cutting as little as possible off the base of the bulb and only just enough off the top to loosen the outer layers. Then cut the onion in half from top to bottom, vertically. Lay the cut side of the onion down on the cutting board and again cut from top to bottom, starting from the right (if right handed). Beautiful crescent moons will appear and each cut has a little of the top as well as of the bottom. Notice that when we cut onions or other round vegetables this way it makes a very balanced cut in comparison to other cuts that are all top or all bottom.

Try also to cut one onion in half moons as described, and spread them on a baking sheet. Take another onion, leave it whole on the same baking sheet, and bake the onions until they are done. The whole onion will need longer cooking time. The half moons will be dry and crunchy whereas the whole onion will be sweet, moist, soft, and hold a lot of warmth.

When we cut vegetables we always seek to balance the sizes, shapes, colors, and flavors. Large cuts are suitable for stews, baked vegetable dishes, and slow cooking styles. Smaller cuts are more delicate and used in lighter cooked soups, stir-fries, and other quicker cooking methods. Try to use even-sized cutting techniques for each dish so that all pieces are cooked and done at the same time.

ROUNDS AND FULL MOONS

Cutting root vegetables into even thick or thin slices creates beautiful rounds or full moons. Slice crosswise beginning at the tip of the root, either thinner or thicker cuts.

HALF MOONS AND QUARTER MOONS

Half moons and quarter moons are done by a similar cutting style as above. Cut root vegetables in half lengthwise. To create half moons, cut these halves crosswise in even slices. To make quarter moons, cut each half down the center again before slicing.

DIAGONALS

Many vegetables such as root vegetables, cabbages, pea pods, beans, and leafy greens can be cut into diagonals by holding the knife at an angle while cutting crosswise. The angle of the blade determines the length of the pieces. Smaller vegetables can be bunched together on top of one another before they are cut. Bigger vegetables such as cabbages need first to be cut in quarters. Cut the stem out of the leafy greens, bunch the stems together, and cut them on a diagonal. Bigger leaves can be cut in half or quarters first. Lay them on top of each other and then cut them diagonally.

MATCHSTICKS

Cutting foods into matchsticks is a technique used with roots and firm round vegetables. Cut the vegetable first into diagonals, then stack the sections and slice them into matchstick-size pieces.

WEDGES

Cutting vegetables into triangles creates wedges. Hold the root vegetables with one hand and the knife at a diagonal angle with the other hand. Roll the vegetables 180 degrees between each cut. The position of the knife stays the same. Squashes can also be cut into wedges; each cut requires a little imagination to get them even in size. Another variation of this is an irregular wedge, cut by rolling the root vegetable 90 degrees after each cut.

FLOWERS

The flower cut is used with root vegetables, especially carrots and parsnips. Cut thin wedges (five works beautifully) on the side of the carrot in its growing direction. Then cut the carrot into rounds.

CUBES

Cutting vegetables into cubes creates a lovely cut especially for soups. The vegetables are first cut crosswise and/or lengthwise into chunks. Stand each piece on its end and cut into 1/4 to 1/2 inch cubes by cutting vertically, then horizontally, and last crosswise. Onions are cubed or diced by first cutting them in half vertically. Each half is sliced from bottom to top, leaving the onion attached to the base of the root. Turn the onion 90 degrees and cut same size slices. The root base can be diced last.

 Explore

Choose one kind of vegetable—for example, carrots. Select a cutting style and cook the vegetable in the different ways described here. Write down your observations of flavors, textures, colors, and so on. Continue the experiment with other cutting styles.

RECTANGLES AND TRIANGLES

Vegetables are cut into rectangles and triangles by first making rounds or chunks about 1 1/2 to 2 inches long, or the desired finished length of the rectangle. Then lay each chunk on its side and cut lengthwise into slices 1/4 inch thick or less. Cutting the rectangles on the diagonal, from one opposing corner to the other, creates triangles.

CHRYSANTHEMUMS

The chrysanthemum style is a beautiful style for decoration. First cut big rounds or chunks about 1 inch thick. Stand the vegetable on the end or base and cut several thin even slices, being careful to keep the slices attached at one end. Turn the vegetable 90 degrees and cut again in equal depth and thickness. Soak the chrysanthemum pieces in ice-cold water to unfold them as flowers.

CRESCENT MOONS

The crescent moon cut is often used with onions and roots. Cut onion or root vegetable lengthwise into halves. Turn the cut side down on the cutting board. Slice crosswise beginning at the tip of the root into thin crescent moon–shaped pieces.

SHAVINGS

Shavings are made in the same way as a pencil is sharpened with a knife. Begin at the bottom of the vegetables, rotating it slightly with each cut. The shaves can be made thin or thick, long or short, by altering the angle of the knife.

Leaving vegetables uncut or almost uncut is a way of preparing the foods in their integrity. Bouquets of broccoli and cauliflower can be separated gently, beans and peas snapped, or whole onions, carrots, and squashes can be cooked as they are.

COOKING STYLES

My choices of pots, pans, and serving bowls are of stainless steel, cast iron, copper, ceramic, simple earthenware, soapstone, glass, or enamel. I cook food on a wood or gas stove since both supply a natural source of heat. It is easy to adjust the heat on a gas stove. There is a big difference in the quality and taste of the foods cooked on a wood stove or a gas stove as opposed to an electric stove or microwave.

I like to use natural wooden utensils, spoons, and chop sticks for stirring and manipulating the food in the pots and pans. They are gentle to the pots and pans and make little or no noise. I minimize the use of electric processors and blenders, although convenient. I prefer hands-on preparation.

The flavor, texture, and quality of foods depend on the cutting styles as well as on the cooking styles used. A raw onion is pungent, crisp, and cooling. A boiled onion has released much of its essence and aroma into the water and therefore has little flavor by itself. A sautéed onion has a strong, powerful taste and is both crunchy and soft at the same time, whereas a baked onion is deliciously sweet, warming, and creamy.

When we cook foods we lift and lighten the dishes or condense and give them weight. As cooks, we are artists, bring different qualities to the meal. We create various flavors and textures as we add salt, water, heat, and time to the foods we cook. We often do this intuitively. On a cold winter day we select hardy vegetables, add water and salt, and let them cook for a long time to make a hot, digestible, warming, nourishing, and strengthening soup. In the summer we would generally use a smaller amount of salt, use less heat, and cook foods in a shorter time.

Different cooking styles bring about different nutritional substances. For example, pickling, fermenting, and serving raw salads will keep the processes of most enzymes and some vitamins active. Light cooking styles, for instance the steaming of broccoli, will inhibit some of these enzymes and some vitamin processes, but will break down cell walls and make the activities of other vitamins and minerals available. Stronger cooking styles, such as baking bread, make a variety of mineral, oils, proteins, and carbohydrates available that otherwise would be inaccessible or indigestible if the grains were eaten raw.

SEASONAL COOKING STYLES

There are many more types of food preparation and combinations than the ones listed in the accompanying diagram. Cooking with locally grown, seasonal whole foods requires imagination to experience their full potential. The diagram of the seasonal styles of cooking is meant to show movement and flexibility in choices of appropriate cooking styles for seasonal foods. Emphasize lighter styles like steaming and water sautéing as well as raw and pressed salads in the summer. Use condensing cooking styles such as long-time cooking and oil sautéing in the autumn, and fried, roasted, and baked dishes in the winter.

Strive also to create a harmonious whole in the choices of cooking styles. For example, baked and fried dishes need to be balanced with just a little raw, lightly

 Explore

How do you feel after eating a carrot?

Take two carrots. Grate one; add a pinch of salt and a few drops of lemon juice. Imagine it is a hot summer day. Sit down and eat the grated carrot. How refreshing and relaxing it feels. This grated raw carrot is just what you needed. Now imagine it is winter. You just came in from the blistering cold, and after eating the grated, raw carrot salad you feel even colder.

Take the other carrot and cut it into chunks. Cook it slowly, using a little water, for 20 minutes and add a pinch of salt. Sit down and enjoy the sweet carrot melting on your tongue. Can you feel its warming, strengthening, and nourishing quality?

pressed, or pickled foods. In the same way, light salads and steamed vegetables need grounding in stronger dishes, even in the summer. Pay attention to the quality of the foods when choosing cooking methods. Deep-reaching, solid roots will become sweeter and more tender when cooked for a longer time, whereas light, delicate leafy greens or blossoms do best with little or no cooking at all.

These styles of cooking can support the daily rhythm as well. Use lighter cooking styles such as boiling, blanching, and steaming in the morning to harmonize with the rising of the day. We can also apply the chart to complement personal health conditions. Notice how we naturally are attracted to stronger contracted foods and cooking styles, like fried fish, when we feel scattered and fragile. Observe how we lean toward lighter foods and cooking styles, like fruits and salads, when we feel irritated or under pressure.

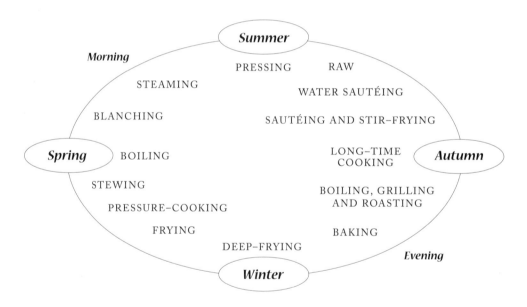

PRESSING AND MARINATING

Raw, pressed, and marinated vegetables are refreshing and wonderful to cool, lighten, and balance dishes that are fried, baked, or prepared with animal foods. These styles of cooking create crispy and crunchy raw side dishes that are served in small portions with the rest of the meal. To prepare raw salads, grate or cut vegetables fine, then make a dressing that goes well with the meal. Pressed salads can be made of heartier vegetables such as cabbage, carrots, beets, onions, radishes, and wild greens.

Cucumbers, Chinese cabbages, and summer squashes also lend themselves well to be pressed.

To prepare pressed salads, finely shave, shred, grate, or cut the vegetables. Mix them with sea salt and let them sit under pressure for 20 minutes to 24 hours. A ceramic crock or bowl with an inside fitting plate and a heavy weight on top work well. During the pressing process water is released from the vegetables. This water can be discarded or used in dressing. When the pressed salad is done, other seasoning such as vinegar and various herbs can be added. Finely cut raw or cooked foods can also be marinated in a seasoning liquid before serving or further cooking.

WATER SAUTÉING

Water sautéing is a method that combines sautéing and boiling. This technique brings warmth, movement, and lightness to the food. Finely cut or grated vegetables are first sautéed in a couple of tablespoons of water over medium heat. Then more water is added to lightly cover the bottom of the pan. A lid is placed on the pot and the vegetables are cooked quickly for a short time. Then seasoning is added; the pot is covered again while the dish finishes cooking for another few minutes. If any juice is left the cover is removed and the liquid is cooked off.

SAUTÉING AND STIR-FRYING

Sautéing vegetables in oil makes them delicious, sweet, and crispy. All kinds of colorful vegetables can be prepared this way successfully. This method of cooking is strengthening and brings gentle movement and warmth to the dish. Cut the vegetables finely; matchsticks, thin slices, and diagonals work well. Add a little oil to a warm frying pan. When the oil begins to sizzle, add the vegetables and a little sea salt. Stir the vegetables gently from time to time with wooden utensils or chopsticks. Sauté the vegetables first on medium heat, then lower the temperature and continue sautéing until the vegetables are done. Cooking time depends on the ingredients and the cutting style used. The vegetables will brighten in color and release an appetizing aroma. The Chinese stir-frying of vegetables is done in a wok using a small amount of oil, high heat, and continuous stirring. This type of cooking style adds warmth and movement as well as lightness to the dish.

LONG-TIME COOKING

The long-time cooking style is ideal to use with firm root vegetables, such as onions and winter squashes, but winter kale and collards are also nutritious cooked this way. This method of cooking is strengthening, calming, centering, and warming.

Vegetables are first cut in large sizes, then layered or placed neatly side-by-side. They are brought to a boil in a small amount of water with a pinch of sea salt and slowly cooked over low heat for about 20 minutes or more. The steam in the pot allows the vegetables to cook slowly and steadily. Seasoning is usually added at the end of the cooking time. These vegetables become sweet, moist, and flavorful. There is little if any cooking liquid left when the dish is finished.

BROILING, GRILLING, AND ROASTING

Broiling, grilling, and roasting give foods a characteristic slightly bitter flavor. These methods are often used to prepare fish, meat, tofu, and tempeh, but vegetables are also delicious cooked this way. Sometimes the ingredients are marinated first. Different sauces can be used before or during the broiling. These styles of cooking are more hardening, drying, and centering. They tend to blacken and sear the exterior of the food and allow soft vegetables to keep their shape without becoming mushy. Grains can be roasted in a dry skillet before they are boiled or pressure cooked to add warmth and flavor.

BAKING

Baking is used especially in the western world. Baking vegetables is as common as baking bread. Hearty root and round ground vegetables such as winter squash are deliciously sweet when baked whole. Baking requires long cooking time. The foods that are to be baked are enclosed in a heated oven so they are surrounded on all sides by dry heat. Baking adds strength as well as warmth to the dish and is condensing and shaping. Many vegetables can be baked whole or cut and placed in covered ceramic or glass dishes. Sometimes oil or water is applied for additional moisture and sealing.

FRYING AND DEEP-FRYING

Frying is a method used to cook foods in oil with little or no stirring and mixing. It is a technique that creates a rich-tasting, dynamic, warming, heavy, and strengthening dish. To pan-fry, cut the ingredients in large pieces or slices. Heat a frying pan. Add a good amount of oil or butter. When the oil or butter sizzles, gently place the foods in the pan and fry them over medium heat. Halfway through the cooking time turn them over and continue the frying. When vegetables, fish, and meats, sometimes coated in a batter, are immersed completely in very hot oil it is call deep-frying. The batter holds the heat and moisture. The food cooks rather quickly when deep-fried.

PRESSURE COOKING

Pressure cooking is mostly reserved for cooking whole grains and beans. Occasionally hardy vegetables can be pressure cooked. The ingredients are locked in a pressure cooker with a tightly fitting lid and cooked with 20 to 30 pounds of pressure. The combination of boiling water, steam, and pressure causes the grains and beans to burst open, which brings out and releases their delicious sweetness and essence. Pressure cooking is intense and can be very satisfying. It creates warmth and brings the inner qualities to the surface. A variation of this cooking style is to place a covered ceramic, glass, or stainless steel pot inside the pressure cooker, much like a double boiler. This is a gentler variation of pressure cooking. The grain kernels are kept still in the pot while being cooked under pressure.

STEWING

Stewing is a method that cooks various foods in a medium amount of boiling water or savory stock. The stew is well seasoned and at times thickened to form a substantial flavorful dish. Foods that are to be stewed can be sautéed or fried first. Stews are often prepared as a one-pot meal served with freshly baked bread or a pot of rice. A well cooked stew causes the ingredients to merge their essence and substances together harmoniously and at the same time keep their individual tastes and qualities. This style of cooking is nourishing, substantial, heartening, and very warming.

BOILING

Boiling is one of the most basic styles of cooking vegetables, beans, and grains. Boiling can be done quickly or take a long time. It is a wetter cooking style that loosens and calms. Vegetables that are boiled for a long time release much of their flavor, substances, and forces to the boiling liquid. This liquid is therefore often served as a soup or used as a broth. Bring a fair amount of water to a boil in a pot before adding the vegetables. If making a soup, add the vegetables that need a longer time to cook first. To make a boiled salad, cook each ingredient by itself or cook the foods that need the same cooking time together. Dark leafy greens like kale and collards are tender and delicious when cooked whole this way because their slight bitterness is released into the water. It is therefore best to discard the cooking liquid afterwards, even though some nutrients are thrown away as well. Beans need to presoak and boil for a long time until completely soft and tender. No salt is added to the water. Kombu sea vegetables help in the process of softening the beans and to enhance their natural flavors. It is an art to boil whole grains well. Generally they need twice

 Explore

What types of foods and cooking styles is your temperament more attracted to?

the amount of water unless creamy porridges are made. Whole grains benefit from being presoaked for 8 hours with a dash of vinegar or juice from fermented foods. When the water comes to a boil, the heat is turned down and the pot is left to simmer gently until the grains are done and all water absorbed.

BLANCHING AND POACHING

Blanching is ideal to retain a fresh deep color and a nice crispy quality. Lighter leafy greens, Chinese cabbage, and very thinly sliced root or round vegetables can all be prepared in this way. This style of cooking is light, opening, and expanding. Bring water to a boil. Immerse the vegetables 15 seconds to 1 minute in rapidly boiling water. Quickly take them out of the water with a strainer and submerge them in cold water if necessary to stop the cooking process. Seasonings or dressings can be added, although blanched vegetables are delicious by themselves. Poaching is a technique used especially when cooking fish. The whole fish or a large piece is submerged in lightly seasoned boiling water. The pot is then removed from the heat or placed over very low heat so that the water doesn't continue to boil. The fish rests in the water until it is done.

STEAMING

Steamed vegetables are light and retain less water. No salt is used in the process, only hot steam to soften the foods. The vegetables become bright in color and often crispy in texture. To prepare the vegetables, cut them into even sizes or leave them whole and cut later. Place a steamer in a pot with about 1/2 to 1 inch of water. Bring the water to a boil before adding the vegetables. Cover the pot and keep the heat medium high. Let the vegetables be bathed in steam for 2 to 10 minutes until they are soft yet tender. Another way to steam foods is to bring 1/2 inch of water to a boil in a pan. Add the vegetables and a pinch of salt. Cover the pot and continue as above.

NATURAL FLAVORS OF LIFE

We season and garnish foods to bring out different qualities in the meal. We add specific calming or stimulating herbs, warming or cooling spices, oils and vinegars, roasted seeds and nuts, natural sweeteners, or mineral-rich sea salt in a subtle way so the foods are not overpowered but retain their natural, distinctive zests and essence. Seasoning is an art and must complement the foods and cooking styles in a harmonious way.

 Explore

Choose a couple of different seasonings. For example, one day eat plenty of raw garlic and on another day eat very salty foods. Observe what happens in your thinking and how you feel afterwards. Compare your observations to one another.

When I season dishes I try first to "taste" with my eyes, ears, and nose instead of with my tongue. Somehow the dishes become more complete that way. When I want to taste the food in my mouth, I ladle a little onto a separate spoon, and wash the spoon in between tasting the different dishes.

Some people are used to hot, spicy or salty, oily foods and might at first be unable to taste all the fine natural flavors of a well-prepared meal. Avoid being tempted to drench the foods in overpowering sauces, fats, salt, and sweeteners. It will not be long before the taste buds will adjust and indulge in the manifold subtle flavors of well-cooked natural whole foods.

FLEXIBILITY IN FOLLOWING RECIPES

When I paint I will at times copy other people's paintings to get new ideas, to understand how the artists work, or to get the right proportions of, for example, a horse. It is similar with recipes. I follow them to find new inspirations or proportions and to get a glimpse into another's work of art.

Cooking is an activity that is alive; it does not conform to measuring and weighing. Yet recipes are expressed in amounts and sizes, cups, pinches, and tablespoons. They are an attempt to let us into the world of creative cooking. It is important, though, that as we follow them we use our own imagination and intuition as well as common sense and change measurements and cooking time whenever appropriate.

While we cook we encounter many variables. The seasons change and so does the environment. Food is living and reflects these changes. We as artists have to adjust and work with this through proper cutting and cooking styles. Notice for example how dry the beans and grains get at times. In the winter or in low humidity we sometimes have to soak beans for 24 hours instead of the usual overnight. Vegetables are often more juicy in the summer and early fall than the same kind of vegetable in the late fall and winter months. We would want to adjust the amount of liquid in our cooking accordingly.

The quality of ingredients is also unique to the season in which they are collected. Sweet tender cabbages and kales picked in the summer are very different from the strong and bitter cabbages and kales harvested in the early fall, and again very different from the delicious fully matured cabbages and kales gathered after the first frost.

Sometimes certain ingredients are not available, or sometimes we intentionally want to exclude or include certain foods. If a recipe calls for honey and I use maple

 Explore

What foods, herbs, and seasonings add a salty, sour, sweet, pungent, and/or bitter flavor to the meal?

syrup or barley malt instead, the color, taste, texture, and quality of the dish will change. Busy bees collect the light and warmth of the summer blossoms to create honey. Maple syrup is a cooked-down concentrate of the vigorous spring sap from tall sturdy maple trees. Dark malt is produced from sprouted golden barley grains. All are sweeteners but each is very unique in its taste, consistency, and qualities.

Notice the difference it makes when salt is added during the cooking time. Cooking without salt relaxes the food; salt added at the end contracts the dish and makes it taste saltier than if the salt was cooked into the foods. A pinch of salt added to roots and fruits in the beginning of their cooking time bring out their sweetness.

We may also pay attention to the cooking style and size of the flame we use. Frying, for example, needs to be done over a medium to higher heat to create crispy surfaces. Heat that is too low brings out the liquid of the vegetables and the dish may become mushy. Some foods all of a sudden become overcooked after just a minute in boiling water, while others dishes benefit from simmering a whole day.

Before we begin cooking the meal we want to decide what dishes take the longest to make. Grains and beans are often soaked a day ahead, and fermented foods have to go through the fermentation process in their own time.

How many persons is the recipe intended for? Here again we have to use our intuition. In the recipes I have created, I usually think of meals for four unless otherwise stated. I serve many dishes and plenty of food at each meal so that each person can satisfy their individual needs. Leftovers in a nourishing broth can create a wonderful tasty soup the following day. How much food to make really depends on how much everyone had to eat earlier in the day and what their activities were. An emotionally tight family member who has been sitting at the computer all day and is just entering the home from a long drive in traffic might find herself reaching for lighter-cooked and richer dishes, while a young adult who has physically worked hard outside may eat several helpings of the fried fish.

When creating meals, be creative and honor simplicity. I often make a quick sketch of what I intend to create before getting all the ingredients together. I ask myself, what kind of meal do I want to make? Do I want to create a warming or cooling, light or substantial meal? In order to create this meal, which dishes will I make and what foods will I need? When I am satisfied with my answers, I bring out the ingredients and start to cook. Other times I start with just the opposite: I select a few ingredients with no specific plan of what to cook. I take before me, for example, salmon, leeks, and cabbage and ask inwardly, "How will these foods want to be cooked? What dishes do they want to become?" By working in this way I take the preparations of the meal out of the realm of ordinary, intellectual thinking. I proceed by adding complementary flavors, textures, colors, and shapes in the form of additional foods, as well as cutting and cooking styles, until a balanced meal is created. I finish up with the details, such as garnishes and pickles to create unity.

CREATING BALANCED MEALS

Take a moment and look at some of the meals I have created for the different seasons. Notice the simplicity and wholesomeness that shines through each dish and each meal. I like to continue the activities in the kitchen in harmony with the seemingly effortless life processes in nature. Like images in a poem, I strive to let each ingredient express itself through the different dishes. The cutting and cooking styles lift and lighten each food or give them weight and strength. Nothing is overpowering or complicated. To mix a lot of ingredients in one dish requires skill. Most often I am left with the same feeling as when I mix too many colors in my painting. The result is either chaotic or a dull, unsatisfying brownish gray. In a balanced meal the ingredients and cutting and cooking styles, as well as the individual dishes, enhance each other in order to create interesting dynamics. As in an engaging painting, an appealing meal consists of both gentle pastel-like dishes as well as colorful dishes bursting with movement and vigor.

The main meal of the day can be a nourishing soup or stew with sourdough bread and sauerkraut. For the most part I create several qualitatively different side dishes around a whole grain dish. I always make sure to include a nourishing soup, whole grains, vegetables (especially leafy greens), protein-rich dishes, high-quality oils or fats, as well as fermented foods. The amount I serve of grains, vegetables, animal foods, oils and fats, desserts, and so on, varies with everyone's needs and the activities of the day, as well as the season. Everything is always changing. Life is dynamic.

In all the recipes I use unrefined, whole, biodynamically grown or otherwise organically grown, and naturally produced foods and beverages. I choose seasonal locally harvested foods whenever possible. Locally grown biodynamic or organic whole grains, beans, vegetable, herbs, and seasonings are available in many health

✿ *Explore*

Find a quiet space within yourself and connect with gratitude in a way that is real for you. Ask yourself, "What foods do or don't support my healthy functioning body, clear mind, stable emotional life, and stamina? What foods do or don't support a healthy local and global economy and ecology?"

food stores. Some places have a grain mill accessible to grind your own fresh flours. It is more difficult to acquire local high-quality fermented foods, fish, raw dairy, eggs, poultry, and other meats from animals who have ranged freely and were fed grass. Much fish today is farm-raised conventionally on pellets. Real raw honey is a rare treasure because most beekeepers add penicillin to the hive, feed the bees sugar, and extract the honey by heat. Most organic eggs, chicken, meat, and dairy come from animals fed on corn in order for them to grow quickly and produce year-round. I go the extra mile to get high-quality foods and support farmers and distributors who sell the high quality.

SOUPS

Soups are a wonderful and satisfying entrance for the meal and set the mood of the dinner. I create light, refreshing, and cooling soups, using cooking styles that lift and loosen with round or upward-growing vegetables, for spring and summer or when the rest of the meal is substantial. I make heartier and warming soups, using stronger cooking styles, emphasizing round and root vegetables during fall and winter days or if the rest of the meal needs grounding.

Some soups are creamy and have a smoothness of color while others soups use ingredients that are crunchy, finely diced, and very colorful. Several soups honor just one or two decoratively cut vegetables in an almost transparent broth. Some soups are like stews where a variety of different ingredients, cut in chunks, almost forms a meal by itself.

I use a light broth or plain, crystal clear water as the liquid for the lighter soups. I make a vegetable stock for heartier and stronger-flavored soups and stews. I cook a stock of meat or fish bones for strengthening and warming soups. Stocks will last in the refrigerator for a week and for months in the freezer. The strength of the soup stock depends on how many ingredients there are and how long the stock has cooked. If a lot of water has evaporated and the stock is very concentrated, I dilute it before cooking with it.

NOURISHING STOCKS COOKED FROM BONES

To make a delicious strengthening stock, cover bones of beef, chicken, or fish (including the heads and tails) with plenty of cold water. Add a couple tablespoons of vinegar and on occasion a tablespoon of green tea placed in a cheesecloth bag. Bring it slowly to a boil. Cover the pot and let the stock simmer for 4 to 12 hours. Let it rest overnight, bring it to a boil the next morning, and continue cooking as long as desired but at least 10 minutes. Strain the liquid from the bones. Vegetables such as carrots, onions, leeks, celery, and herbs such as rosemary, oregano, thyme, and bay leaf can be added to the stock and simmered along for the last hour. Solidified fats can be removed after the stock has cooled down.

VEGETABLE STOCK

Cooking a variety of vegetable trimmings with whole vegetables makes a lighter, very nourishing and flavorful vegetable stock. Use especially leeks, carrots, celery root, cabbage stems (use only a small amount from the kale family), onions, winter squashes, and celery. Place the vegetables and trimmings in plenty of cold water with a 3- to 5-inch piece of kombu sea vegetable. The sea vegetables are the bones of the sea and a natural flavor enhancer. Simmer the stock for one hour and strain it before using it.

LIGHT SEA VEGETABLE STOCK

A nourishing but neutral very light stock is made by placing a 3- to 5-inch piece of kombu sea vegetable in a quart of cold water for 10 to 20 minutes. Remove the kombu and use it in other dishes—for example, when cooking beans.

WHOLE GRAINS AND BREADS

The sun-ripened golden grains are the heart of my meals. When prepared well, grains have a delicious, sweet flavor. I carefully pick out any debris before I cook them. Then I wash the whole grains gently by covering them with water. I run my clean hands through the grains a few times before I strain the water off. I do this until the rinsing water is clear. Afterwards I add the cooking liquid, which most often is plain water. Stocks and spices are fun additions to the cooking liquid only once in a while. For digestibility, I soak the grains in slightly warmed water with an added dash of liquid from natural fermented foods. I use sourdough for bread making. Most often I make whole wheat bread, but I also make sourdough breads with combinations of rice, oats, millet, rye, barley, and corn flour. When using grains other than wheat, I use less flour. The dough is moist and can be spooned into the baking pans. Well-done sourdough bread is sweet and only slightly sour. Yeasted and chemically leavened (baking powder and baking soda) breads are lighter and quicker to make occasionally but no comparison in quality.

WHEAT is a flour grain. Hard winter wheat is best for breads and muffins.

Softer varieties are better for pasties, and durum wheat for noodles and pastas, bulgur, and couscous.

BROWN RICE is a versatile and delicious grain. It can be cooked whole or milled into flour. Short grain brown rice is a harder variety whereas medium and long grain brown rice are lighter and softer. Sweet rice is sticky and more glutinous.

OAT is a cereal of the north. Rich and heartening, this nourishing grain lends itself well to warming porridges and soothing creamy soups.

MILLET is enjoyed around the world cooked whole but sometimes milled. The common American type is golden yellow whereas many Asian varieties are red.

RYE is a hard, chewy cereal grain cultivated mainly in Europe where it is used in making the delicious sourdough rye bread. In Denmark rye bread is served at almost every meal.

BARLEY is a hardy cereal grain used in baked goods, soups, and porridges. Pearled barley has undergone a refining process and has been husked and hulled.

CORN comes in many varieties, traditionally cooked with wood ash. Flint corn has hard kernels and matures early. Dent corn has softer kernels than flint corn, matures later, and is easier to grind. It is used to make cornmeal, polenta, and tortillas. Blue corn is similar to yellow flint corn and has a slightly sweeter flavor.

At times I also use teff, quinoa, and amaranth, native to South Africa and to Central and South America. They are mainly used whole, prepared with other grains and vegetables. Buckwheat, grown in the cooler parts of the world, is best known roasted as kasha or ground into flour and used in pancakes and noodles.

SEASONAL VEGETABLES AND FRUITS

When cooking a main meal, I make several side dishes of freshly cooked, locally grown seasonal vegetables. I use a wide selection of roots, leafy greens, fruits, and seeds in appropriate proportions, using a variety of cutting and cooking styles. I carefully clean all the vegetables in cold water using a vegetable brush whenever needed. I rub the vegetables gently and try to leave the peel intact. Sometimes I cut the vegetables open to rinse them inside, as with leeks. I trim any bruised or bad spots neatly around tops, bottoms, and stems.

For the most part I select fresh seasonal fruits and vegetables locally grown. There are exceptions. In the winter I will buy leafy greens grown elsewhere when my own supply from the garden runs out. Occasionally I purchase other fresh out-

 Explore

Pick a meal from the cooking section. What parts of plants are used in the meal? Which dishes and ingredients contain quality oils? What different cooking styles are used and what is the general "mood" of the meal? Are all the five major flavors represented? What raw, pickled, or cultured foods are served with the meal?

Do the colors, cooking and cutting styles complement each other? What garnishes are used?

of-season vegetables, like a cauliflower shipped in from sunny California or other parts of the world. At times I use frozen peas and corn for variation and color in the meal. Every now and then I find tropical fruits in a dressing or dessert appropriate additions to the meal even though I live in a temperate climate. Once in a while I use vegetables from the nightshade family such as tomato, bell peppers, eggplants, and potatoes. The nightshades are very different from other vegetable plants and are mainly suited for medicinal uses. I cook with only a very small amount of vegetables from the sea. All in all I prefer using vegetables and fruits that are grown locally in the season they are available.

ANIMAL FOODS, DAIRY, AND BEANS

I serve at least one side dish that include beans (lentils, chickpeas, etc.), bean products (tofu and tempeh), fresh or frozen fish (preferably wild or farm-raised organically), free-range poultry, eggs, grass-pastured meat (including organ meat), or raw, unhomogenized, cultured dairy products like yogurt and raw cheese. I rarely cook with dairy products, except for butter, since the pasteurization completely changes the quality and makes them difficult to digest.

Vegetables are formed directly by forces and substances outside themselves. These forces extend into the starry realm and the depth of the earth. Animals are very different from plants. The outside earthly and cosmic forces are turned inward in the creation of internal organs and unique bodily systems, which enable the animals to move around independently in order to fulfill their desires and impulses. Animal foods are much more condensed and bring very different qualities to the meal than vegetable quality foods. Dairy can be imagined as a food somewhere between vegetable and animal foods. In order to do justice to the world of animals, a separate book must be dedicated to the life of all the fascinating land, water, and air creatures, how and where they live, and how to cook with them. Fresh, unprocessed or cultured dairy, fish, or animal foods have been part of many different cultures' dietary heritage. To either exclude or include animal foods in the diet and to decide the appropriate proportions is a personal choice that must be seriously considered by each individual.

Many of the recipes in this book contain animal foods, especially fish. If you choose to omit them from your diet, make sure to include high-quality oils and raw cultured dairy along with dishes that include sturdy downward-growing roots and strengthening cooking methods. When you include animal foods in your meals,

 Explore

Sit down in a quiet space. Ask yourself, "What amount of animal food do I and each of the family members need?" Listen to the feeling that arises and insights that come to you.

Your needs will change, so keep checking in with yourself from time to time. Stay flexible and be willing to explore.

make sure the animals have been pasture-fed (healthy fish need wild sea grasses as well) and free-ranged. Garnish with scallions when cooking with eggs; use a small amount of garlic, onion; or grated radishes with most meats; use lemon with light, white fish and mustard with fatty red meat fish, like tuna and salmon.

When cooking beans, I add a small amount of kombu sea vegetables for flavor and digestibility as well as spices to bring about movement. Soybeans are best only eaten in the form of miso, tempeh, and occasionally tofu seasoned with soy sauce.

OILS, FATS, SEEDS, AND NUTS

Healthy oils and fats are very important ingredients in the meal. They are naturally present in grains, beans, fish, meats, seeds, and nuts. I use high-quality unrefined, cold-pressed extra virgin olive, freshly pressed dark sesame oil, freshly churned butter, cream, and other high-quality animal fats. I often sprinkle freshly ground flax seeds, soaked and roasted sesame or sunflower seeds, and various freshly shelled and soaked nuts on grains, salads, and desserts. Soaking the nuts and seeds make them more digestible. For most of the year I supplement one meal a day with a small amount of cod liver oil and fish oil as well.

SEASONINGS

Herbs and spices originate from all parts of a plant: the roots, bark, leaves, blossoms, fruits, and seeds. Their abundant fragrances and flavors, tastes and aromas fill our senses and alter the quality of the dishes. In my garden I grow rosemary, thyme, oregano, dill, parsley, scallions, chives, sage, coriander, marjoram, chamomile, chervil, basil, caraway, mint, tarragon, and garlic. All winter I pick many of these herbs fresh from plants growing in pots on my enclosed sun-bathed porch. Other natural seasonings that I use regularly are naturally fermented apple cider, rice or balsamic vinegars, fresh cold-pressed extra virgin olive oil, fresh dark-roasted sesame oil, cultured butter, zesty mustards, sun-dried unrefined sea salt, and traditionally fermented and aged tamari and tamari soy sauce (shoyo), miso, umeboshi plums, and umeboshi vinegars. I add small amounts of sea vegetables, like kombu, as a bean tenderizer and natural flavor enhancer of the whole foods. The ways in which I prepare vegetables and grains bring out their natural sweetness. The whole meal is therefore naturally sweet. The other major flavors, salty, pungent, sour, and bitter, are represented without dominating delicate flavors naturally found in whole foods.

Explore

Blend one tablespoon of flaxseeds and pumpkin seeds with a dash of sea salt in a little coffee grinder. Sprinkle this flaxseed condiment on grain and vegetable dishes.

CULTURED AND FERMENTED FOODS

I serve some kind of fermented or raw food with each meal. Naturally fermented and cultured foods are an exceptional way to prepare different ingredients and some of the most important side dishes or condiments in our diet. They are often overlooked or not mentioned when we describe what we had for dinner, and yet they are pivotal in creating a well-balanced nutritious meal. They add a bounty of nourishing and life-promoting substances and forces, almost miraculous curative properties, and a wealth of color, flavors, and shapes. They increase the appetite, stimulate the digestion, and make any simple meal festive and satisfying.

It is an old art to make naturally fermented and cultured foods. They are prepared without the direct use of fire or heat and were an excellent way to preserve food for the times when fresh produce was not available. People of all cultures enjoy fermented and cultured foods. The Greeks pickle olives, Germans turn cabbages into appetizing sauerkraut, and the Japanese transform green, immature plums into the tasty medicinal umeboshi plums. Grains and beans are cultured in the Far East, creating the now well-known nutritious miso and tamari soy sauce. Indonesian families culture soybeans to create tempeh. In many places of the world people ferment grains or fruit into wine, beer, or vinegars. Everywhere flours of various grains are traditionally leavened with sourdough to create delicious breads. From Scandinavia and Russia come the tasty drinks kvass and kombucha, which keep young and old healthy and satisfy the need for fresh foods throughout the long winters. Many societies in the world culture the dairy of animals to make yogurt, butter, kefir, and cheese.

The most significant aspects of these foods are found in the process in which they are made. The fermentation or culturing process is more important than the foods that are fermented. When green cabbage is shredded and placed under pressure with a little sea salt, the liquids are extracted from the cabbage. In this liquid, ethereal life forces and gases are freed. While the cabbage mixture increases in temperature, chemical interactions take place and substances transform. The matured and finished sauerkraut has become an individual unique food with an inner liveliness, flavor, and aroma completely its own. A whole new product has been created consisting of magical living microorganisms and an abundance of nutritious substances and forces. The microorganisms in the sauerkraut, the lacto bacilli, not only create flavors and textures but they also produce an environment wherein unwanted bacteria cannot live and therefore the foods are preserved instead of rotting.

It is relatively simple to ferment or pickle vegetable foods. Most can be ready in a few hours or in a few days while others, like miso, can take years to mature. The different pickles and fermented foods have different properties, effects, flavors, and consistency. Some are more sour, some salty, some crispy, and some soft; some are strengthening and warming, others loosening and cooling. If, for example, a heavier meal is served with fried foods and well-cooked dishes, a lighter, cooling fermented food is preferred to balance the meal.

DESSERTS

Most of the time I create a balanced meal that is complete and satisfying without a dessert. A balanced meal in itself is naturally sweet, colorful, and flavorful and includes a variety of textures, cooking styles, and cutting techniques. Adding fermented foods and various condiments to the meal brings all the dishes to a unified whole.

Once in a while I make a dessert or sweet beverage using natural processed sweeteners. Sweeteners are very concentrated (forty quarts of maple sap make one quart of syrup) so I use them in small amounts. My favorite sweeteners are maple syrup, sorghum, barley malt, rice syrup, raw or cooked fruit, and fruit juices or concentrate. I use raw, unpasteurized honey in dressings and dishes that do not need to be heated.

THE FINISHING TOUCH

Serving the meal is the presentation of our artwork. Arrange the individual plates beautifully with all the dishes together side-by-side, or use decorative simple serving bowls. Give the foods a chance to show their individual beauty, colors, and forms by displaying them on a plain background, leaving plenty of space around for them to "breathe." How beautifully a natural glazed ceramic plate complements a simple dish of steamed bright green broccoli with a creamy light dressing!

When we serve the meal, we can think of it as a whole and at the same time allow each dish to proclaim its own glory. Imagine a harmonious conversation taking place between each dish. Let them complement each other in color, shape, and taste to create a balanced whole. Once in a while serve the meal in courses or a few dishes at a time, so that they really can be seen and enjoyed on their own.

Ideally serve every dish freshly made. When I serve leftovers I make sure to take them out of the refrigerator in time for them to warm to room temperature.

Sometimes I reheat them lightly in order to reactivate the forces in the food. In my experience most vegetable dishes are best not reheated.

Garnishes bring liveliness and movement to the meal. Besides a sprig of fresh herbs, I garnish with finely cut watercress and other green vegetables, radishes, celery leaves, carrots, and raw onions. I cut decorative shapes out of fruits and vegetables (carrot flowers, radish chrysanthemum, or apple slices), or use a little grated daikon, fried bread cubes, roasted seeds and nuts, ginger, wedges of lemon, orange peel, horseradish, and colorful edible flowers (dandelion, nasturtium, borage, violets) for garnishes. Used appropriately, garnishes add beauty and balance to the meal.

Create a simple, peaceful, and lovely atmosphere around the dinner table. Remove any clutter and clean the eating space, even if dining alone. Set and decorate an attractive table using a tablecloth or place mats, cloth napkins, nice serving dishes, glasses and plates. Place just a few fresh flowers, pretty rocks, dried or fresh leaves, a potted plant, or candles on the table to set a seasonal mood. Do it subtly. This is the frame around our artwork, the meal we have prepared.

Now let us pause and delight in this co-creation with nature before we sit down to eat.

AT THE TABLE

Eating a meal together is one of the highest social acts of communion. The meal we have prepared so diligently is offered freely in an atmosphere of warmth and received in gratitude. With quiet joyous conversation around the table, we share the impressions of the day and listen carefully with interest. Intimately we delight in each other and the gifts of nature.

GRACE

When two or more are gathered together in unison around a meal, something special is allowed to happen. This special mood and feeling could be described as being bestowed by grace. The word grace comes from the Latin grazia, which means "the divine gift of radiance, which brings joy to the heart."

At the table, before I begin to eat, I settle myself and move into the region of my heart. Centering in the realm of the heart has a quality of reverence. I enter into this space between the physical world and the invisible world of spiritual forces. It is possible to simultaneously be fully present in both realms. I feel it in a very bodily way as a subtle and gentle force of beauty, light, and warmth. In this region of the heart, the boundaries of the body expand, my perception opens, and both worlds emerge vividly and intensely. Here in this living space I feel "the divine gift of radiance which brings joy to the heart."

I may say a prayer or express my gratitude for life, my family and friends, and all the forces, beings, and people that helped in getting this meal to me, either silently while in the realm of the heart or out loud. When I am with children I sing a joyous song or say a seasonal verse. I contemplate silently how the nourishing rain, the

 Explore

Contemplate these words of Johann Wolfgang Goethe: "Take care of your body with steadfast fidelity. The soul must see things through these eyes alone, and if they are dim, the whole world is clouded."

Explore

Cut a pear in half and
eat the first half.

Now savor the other half of the
pear. Smell its deliciousness, feel
the heaviness and the plumpness
of the form. Bite it so that your
teeth sink into the ripe flesh of
the pear ever so slowly, and feel
the juice running in your mouth.
Chew it thoroughly and mix
the bite with your saliva. Notice
the softness and possibly a little
crunchiness of the pear. Let your
tongue play with it in your mouth,
as you taste all the flavors. Is
there a little bitterness too?

What is the pear telling you?
Could the pear's deepest
wish be to really be known
in its entire splendor?

warmth belonging to the sun, the worms, the farmers, and the loving hands of the
people who cooked the meal all contributed to the creation of the food I have in
front of me. Appreciation streams through my being in preparation for receiving the
"sacrifice" all foods make, whether of vegetable or animal origin. The wheat kernels
have given their lives to the flourmill and become bread as nourishment for me. As I
eat the bread, the grains "resurrect" in me and become part of the processes that are
creating a human being in order for me to fulfill my tasks and meet my destiny in life.
I sense the responsibilities that clearly follow. There is much to be thankful for every
day at every meal, here together!

SAVORING THE FOOD

As I begin to eat, I take my time and really savor the food with all my senses. I rejoice
in the smoothness of the cooked onion, the solid roundness of the carrots, and the
glorious array of colors on my plate. I delight in the numerous scents that rise from
the meal and feel the warmth or coolness each individual dish creates. I taste all the
various flavors—the gentle sweetness of the whole meal, the subtle sour and bitter or
pungent and salty flavors of the side dishes and garnishes. Sometimes I can separate
them, other times they blend harmoniously together. I admire the beauty of the food
and how it came into being, how each was created of the heavenly and earthly forces.
I savor the wholeness and holiness of the meal.

As I chew my food thoroughly fifty, a hundred, or two hundred times, I notice
the different changes that happen to the textures, temperature, and the flavors. I
taste the sweetness the whole grains create as they dissolve in my mouth. This is the
most delicious taste I can imagine.

I swallow the food when it is completely liquidized. I imagine how the organs, in
their own quiet ways, continue "tasting" and digesting the ingested meal. Intuitively
they sense the creative forces that live in the foods as a result of the processes that
brought them into being, as well as the forces living in each dish as a result of the
cutting and cooking styles I chose. I envision these forces emancipated and transformed as the foods slowly are savored throughout my being. Eating is a most sacred
act, a communion between heaven and earth, celebrated within as we break bread
together.

DIGESTION, A CELEBRATION OF LIFE

The processes of digestion are a mystery, so wonderful and quite inconceivable. What is most amazing to recognize is that our human substances are very unique and completely different from what is found anywhere in nature. The minerals and protein in our bones and blood are entirely different from the minerals and proteins we find in other parts of nature. Calcium inside the human body is unlike any calcium outside of it. Foods and substances that enter the human body must be completely digested and broken down beyond anything physical. Then will each individual soul/spirit, in co-creation with other majestic spiritual forces, fashion its own distinctive blood, muscles, and bones. Everything that crosses the human threshold must undergo a total transformation! The substances in the food we eat are not directly building blocks, as often imagined, but entirely changed and permeated with our own life. Instead we can imagine that the substances we eat stimulate certain processes and attract various spiritual forces that condense into the individual physical human being. The processes of human digestion are a complete dissolving of the food and its forces, which stimulate a unique recondensing into living, human bodily matter and activities. Digestion is a miracle and a celebration of life.

 Explore

Remember how material substances are densified spirit-light, how they were born out of spiritual warmth, manifesting as gaseous substances, and condensed further into liquids and solids?

Picture the opposite processes taking place during the digestion of the meal. Imagine some of the life forces and substances of the food you just chewed, and thereby made liquid, completely dissolve back into spirit warmth and light. Along with other cosmic substances, imagine your individuality assisting in recondensing these cosmic substances into human activities, blood, and tissue.

STARTING NEW—
COOKING FOR SPRING

After the stillness and harshness of winter, invigorating, warmer winds fill the air, carrying chattering songs of returning birds and the subtle fragrance of fresh dark humus. Streams swell and rush to the rivers as the sap in the trees is lifted to the outmost branch. The light becomes stronger and brighter, welcoming the greening of the fields and leafing of the bushes. The earth once more exhales its life forces. The introversion of winter has passed. Beauty seems to well forth from all reaches of the cosmos. I greet the world with joy and anticipation as it sprouts with new life.

Lovely tulips, Easter lilies, and crocuses adorn the garden edges with the brilliant colors I have been waiting for all winter. While I walk attentively among the newly dug garden beds these lovely early spring mornings, I sense a feeling of being very close to busy nature-beings scuttling around the dewy plants. I try to be present in such a way that is least disturbing to the activities going on there.

I notice how rapidly the radishes have grown next to the outwardly spreading leaf lettuce in the moist, loose soil. The bed looks lush and abundant compared to the neighboring, newly seeded plots. I become aware of the small grass-like sprouts of leeks, onions, and carrots, thinking that they have a long journey ahead of them. The recently transplanted kale, collard, and mustard greens are still far apart as they reach and spread their thin leaves horizontally in the morning sun. Soon tender, young leafy greens will be available for spring meals. The burdocks I left in the ground last fall have sent up shoots to let me know of their readiness to be dug up. Dandelion greens spiral up and out around a beautiful bright yellow sun-like blossom. The oregano, sage, thyme, and chives that wintered in the garden are in full growth. Their fragrances cling to my hands as I pluck their foliage. Everywhere plants are leafing out, growing and becoming. The promise of a plentiful harvest rings throughout the garden.

 Explore

Gather whole stalks of nettles before they flower. Hang each plant to dry, upside-down, in a well-ventilated room and in the shade. Let them dry completely. Store them in paper bags. To make a nourishing infusion, place one cup coarsely cut nettle stalks and leaves in a quart jar. Pour boiling water over and let it steep for 4 hours. Strain the liquid and enjoy the infusion hot or cold.

SPRING MENUS

These spring menus encourage new beginnings and lightness of body and soul. They are colorful, delicious, and nourishing. Each meal is beautiful, an artwork in itself, simple in its form, and interesting to make.

EARLY SPRING MENU

Consommé with Snap Peas and Chives
Rice with Black Olives
Broiled Salmon with Thyme
Steamed Broccoli with Honey Mustard Dressing
Sautéed Radishes and Greens with Sesame Seeds
Lemon Carrot Salad

CELEBRATION OF SPRING MENU

Light Vegetable Soup with Dill
Crunchy Rice and Wheat Berries with Sesame Salt
Herbed Tofu Rolls with Ginger Sauce
Paprika Eggs with Scallions and Miso Mayonnaise
Sautéed Scallops in Garlic
Butter Drizzled Steamed Asparagus
Rosemary Stuffed Mushrooms
Spring Burdock and Nettles with Cilantro
Arame Sea Vegetables with Orange Rind
Wild Green Sauté
Pressed New Radishes

LATE SPRING MENU

Barley Mushroom Soup with Scallions
Green Arugula Salad with Sweet Vinegar Miso Dressing
Oatmeal Cookies
Almond Yogurt Dessert

EARLY SPRING MENU

Consommé with Snap Peas and Chives
Rice with Black Olives
Broiled Salmon with Thyme
Steamed Broccoli with Honey Mustard Dressing
Sautéed Radishes and Greens with Sesame Seeds
Lemon Carrot Salad

The rice is cooked in a way that can omit soaking ahead of time. While cooking the grains, prepare all vegetables and make the dressing. Create each vegetable dish one by one, and end with the soup. When everyone is seated, broil the salmon.

CONSOMMÉ WITH SNAP PEAS AND CHIVES

This clear soup is deliciously light and beautiful when served in decorative ceramic bowls. Instead of snap peas use small quartered onions, wild onions, or scallions.

1 quart soup stock (see Soups)
1 cup snap peas, cut diagonal or left whole
1/2 to 1 tablespoon sea salt
Black pepper to taste
2 tablespoons chives, minced
4 dandelion flowers for garnish

Strain the stock well and bring to a boil. If the stock is very strong, add water so the soup will be flavorful, but not overpowering.

Add snap peas and let simmer for 1-2 minutes.

Season with salt and pepper, then let the soup simmer for another minute.

Serve immediately in individual bowls and garnish with chives and dandelion flowers.

RICE WITH BLACK OLIVES

The light-colored rice and dark olives contrast each other appetizingly. Use freshly pickled olives or fresh olives packed in oil. At times substitute the water with a light soup stock.

2 cups short grain brown rice
4 cups spring or well water
1 teaspoon vinegar or liquid from cultured foods
1/4 teaspoon sea salt
1/2 cup black calamari olives, drained, pitted and sliced

Rinse and drain the rice.

In a heavy-bottom pot place rice, water, and one teaspoon vinegar, or liquid from cultured foods.

Bring water and rice slowly to a boil over low heat, for about 20 minutes. Add salt and cover. Insert a flame tamer between the pot and heat source. Let it simmer for 50-60 minutes.

Remove the pot from heat and let the rice rest for 10 minutes.

Use a wooden spoon to transfer the rice to a serving dish.

Garnish decoratively with olives. Cover with a cotton cloth or rice mat until ready to serve.

BROILED SALMON WITH THYME

Salmon is nutritious and deliciously fatty. Cod, catfish, or tuna can be cooked instead. Watch the broiling closely so that the fish cooks just enough to make it tender but not dry.

> *2-4 salmon filets*
> *4-6 tablespoons extra virgin olive oil*
> *4 pinches of sea salt*
> *1-2 tablespoon fresh thyme, minced, and 4 sprigs for decoration*

Rinse the salmon filets and dry them on paper towel. Lightly brush filets with olive oil and place on an oiled cookie sheet that fits the broiler.

Broil filets 7-12 minutes depending on size. Turn over and broil for another 5 minutes, or until the surface is slightly brown.

Sprinkle the remaining olive oil, a pinch of sea salt and fresh thyme on top of each filet and serve immediately. Decorate the plate with sprigs of thyme.

STEAMED BROCCOLI WITH HONEY MUSTARD DRESSING

Broccoli florets add a lovely, strong green color when steamed. Served with mustard dressing this dish becomes slightly pungent, sweet, and refreshing, which complements the fish and rice well.

2 cups medium broccoli florets

2 tablespoons unpasteurized raw honey

2 tablespoons mustard, stone ground

4 tablespoons extra virgin olive oil (optional)

1/2 teaspoon sea salt

Trim the stems of broccoli and cut florets from the stem up, gently separating heads. Make sure they are all about the same size.

Steam the broccoli florets in a steamer, or layered in a pot with 1/2 inch water, for 5-7 minutes. The broccoli should be tender, yet crisp. Immediately place the broccoli on a serving dish to cool.

Make the dressing by stirring honey, mustard, oil and salt together in a cup.

Just before serving, pour some of the dressing decoratively over the broccoli.

SAUTÉED RADISHES AND GREENS WITH SESAME SEEDS

Radishes are commonly eaten uncooked. Experience how delicious they are when lightly sautéed with a dash of tamari soy sauce. The pungent flavor and cooling nature of the raw radish disappears. The texture becomes soft and moist. The sesame seeds add a light bitterness to the meal.

1/4 cup sesame seeds
2 tablespoons extra virgin olive oil
20 round radishes, trimmed and quartered
1 cup radish greens, washed and cut into 1-inch pieces
1 tablespoon water
1-2 tablespoons tamari soy sauce

Soak the sesame seeds for 5-10 minutes, and then drain them thoroughly.

Heat a stainless steel frying pan and add seeds. Dry-roast the seeds until they are easily squeezed between thumb and ring finger. Stir constantly and rhythmically. When done, set them aside in a bowl to cool.

Pour oil into a lightly heated frying pan. Add radishes and sauté for a few minutes.

Add the green tops and water. It may not be necessary to add additional water if enough rinsing water remained on the greens. Cover the pan with a lid and let it simmer for 2 minutes.

Pour off any extra liquid.

Lightly season with tamari soy sauce and simmer for 1 minute. Place the radishes and greens in a serving dish.

Before serving, add roasted seeds and mix well.

LEMON CARROT SALAD

This bright, delicious orange salad lifts the meal. It is satisfying, zesty, and quite refreshing.

2 medium-size carrots
A pinch of sea salt
Juice of 1/2 to 1 lemon
Sprigs of parsley for garnish

Grate the carrots on a fine grater.

Add sea salt, season with lemon juice, and blend well.

Garnish with sprigs of parsley.

CELEBRATION OF SPRING MENU

Light Vegetable Soup with Dill

Crunchy Rice and Wheat Berries with Sesame Salt

Herbed Tofu Rolls with Ginger Sauce

Paprika Eggs with Scallions and Miso Mayonnaise

Sautéed Scallops in Garlic

Butter Drizzled Steamed Asparagus

Rosemary Stuffed Mushrooms

Spring Burdock and Nettles with Cilantro

Arame Sea Vegetables with Orange Rind

Wild Green Sauté

Pressed New Radishes

This festive meal offers a variety of spring flavors. Soak the rice and wheat berries for 6 to 8 hours. Make the tofu roll first so it has time to cool. Prepare the stuffed mushrooms but wait until the last minute to bake them. Cook the rice, arame, and burdock dish while steaming the asparagus. Finish the rest of the dishes one at a time.

LIGHT VEGETABLE SOUP WITH DILL

Frying vegetables before cooking them in a soup brings out their sweetness and creates a more warming dish. Use the last of your winter vegetables for this soup.

2 teaspoons dark roasted sesame oil or extra virgin olive oil

1/2 cup leeks, washed well, cut thinly on the diagonal

1/2 cup carrot, cut in fine matchsticks

1 quart water or light soup stock

1-2 tablespoons barley or rice miso to taste

4 tablespoons of dill, cut very fine

Heat a soup pot, add oil and sauté the leeks for a minute. Add carrots and sauté for 2 minutes.

Add water or light stock and let simmer for 7 minutes.

Dilute and puree miso in a little soup water before adding it to the pot. Let it simmer a few minutes.

Serve the soup in individual bowls garnished with fresh dill.

CRUNCHY RICE AND WHEAT BERRIES WITH SESAME SALT

Wheat is mainly used in bread making. Soaking and cooking rice and wheat together creates a delicious chewy dish. Sesame salt adds a slight salty and bitter flavor. Pressure cooking brown rice is delicious and strengthening. The grains burst open with sweetness and flavor. Substitute wheat berries with other grains.

2 cups short or medium grain brown rice
1/2 cup whole wheat berries
3 1/4 cups warmed water
1 teaspoon vinegar or liquid from cultured foods
2 pinches sea salt

Rinse the rice and wheat. Soak the grains in the water with vinegar for 8 hours.

Place the grains, soaking water and sea salt in a pressure cooker. Put the lid on tightly and bring the pot to full pressure. Use a flame tamer under the pressure cooker. Reduce heat and maintain pressure for 40 minutes.

Turn off heat and let the pressure come down slowly. Remove the lid and place the rice gently in a serving bowl. Cover with a bamboo mat or cotton towel until ready to serve.

SESAME SALT

1 cup sesame seeds
1 tablespoon sea salt

Wash the seeds and soak for 5 minutes in water. Drain thoroughly.

Preheat a large skillet. Dry-roast the seeds over medium heat until the seeds can be crushed easily between the thumb and ring finger. Keep the seeds moving.

Place the hot seeds and salt in a mortar. Grind the seeds and sea salt together using rhythmical, even circular movements. The sesame salt is done when 90 % of the seeds are crushed. Serve in a separate bowl and store in a tight glass container.

HERBED TOFU ROLLS WITH GINGER SAUCE

Tofu is made from soybeans. It is a refined product and has a cooling nature. In this recipe, the tofu is served with a ginger sauce that stimulates warmth and circulation. Umeboshi vinegar is the brine of the fermented medicinal Japanese umeboshi plums.

3/4 pound firm tofu
2 tablespoons umeboshi vinegar
3 tablespoons fresh oregano, sage, marjoram and chives
1 bamboo mat

In a mixing bowl crumble the tofu finely and mix with the umeboshi.

Cut the herbs very fine and blend them into the tofu mixture.

Place a bamboo mat on the cutting board with bamboo twigs going from left to right. Lay the tofu mixture firmly on the mat, leaving 1 inch free at the top and bottom. Fold the mat tightly around tofu mixture to make a roll. Secure the roll with rubber bands. Tuck the ends in.

Boil 1 inch of water in a large pot with a steamer. Steam the roll in the covered pot over medium heat for 10 minutes.

Let the roll cool completely before removing the mat. Slice into 1/2 inch pieces and arrange decoratively on a serving dish.

GINGER SAUCE

2 tablespoons freshly grated ginger
3 tablespoons tamari soy sauce
3 tablespoons water

Grate the ginger and squeeze juice into a small flat dish. Mix with tamari soy sauce and water. Serve the dipping sauce with the tofu roll.

PAPRIKA EGGS WITH SCALLIONS AND MISO MAYONNAISE

Fresh eggs in the spring from free-range chickens are delicious. The yolk is deep golden and rich, much different than the pale yolk of corn-fed chickens.

6 fresh farm eggs
6-8 tablespoons mayonnaise (see recipe)
1 tablespoon white miso
Pepper to taste
1 teaspoon paprika
2 scallions, cut fine on a diagonal

Place the eggs in a saucepan and cover them with cold water. Bring the water to a boil and simmer for 4 minutes. Drain off the water and rinse in cold water to cool down. Peel the eggs. If the eggs are really fresh, use a spoon to get the shell off. Cut the eggs in half, lengthwise.

Stir mayonnaise, miso and pepper together. Add a teaspoon of miso mayonnaise to each half. Serve garnished with paprika and scallions.

(See recipe on the next page)

MAYONNAISE

Most store-bought mayonnaises are made with refined oils to secure a light taste. Make your own mayonnaise with extra virgin olive oil.

1 egg
1 tablespoon vinegar
1 teaspoon salt
1 tablespoon mustard
1 cup cold pressed extra virgin olive oil

Place the egg, vinegar, salt and mustard in a blender. Blend for 20 seconds. On low speed, slowly add a little oil. Continue until the mayonnaise thickens. Store the mayonnaise in a glass jar with a tight lid and refrigerate.

 ## SAUTÉED SCALLOPS IN GARLIC

Big jumbo shrimp can be used instead of, or with, the scallops. Use fresh scallops or frozen. Thaw the scallops or shrimp overnight or submerged in cold water for about 7 minutes. Leaving them in the bag keeps the flavor in the scallops or shrimp.

4 tablespoons extra virgin olive oil or fresh butter for sautéing
1 pound scallops thawed
1 teaspoon dried garlic granulate or 2 fresh garlic cloves, finely minced
Wooden toothpicks
Slices of lemon for garnish

Heat the oil, not too hot, in a frying pan. Add the scallops and sauté for 3 minutes while stirring gently.

Sprinkle garlic over the scallops and sauté for another minute.

Place a toothpick in each scallop and arrange decoratively in a serving dish. Pour any oil left in pan over the scallops and garnish with slices of lemon.

BUTTER DRIZZLED STEAMED ASPARAGUS

The first asparagus of the year are delicious by themselves drizzled with a little organic butter or extra virgin olive oil and sea salt.

1 small handful asparagus
Fresh butter (see Late Winter Menu) or extra virgin olive oil
Sea salt to taste

Rinse and trim the asparagus. Cut the asparagus into halves if they are too large to fit into the pot.

Boil one inch water in a large pot. Place a steamer inside. On the steamer, lay the biggest asparagus first, and the rest on top. Cover the pot and steam over medium heat for 10 minutes, or until the asparagus are soft and tender.

Immediately transfer to a serving dish. Drizzle oil or butter and sprinkle sea salt on the asparagus while they are still hot. Serve right away.

ROSEMARY STUFFED MUSHROOMS

The stuffed mushrooms can be made in advance, but need to be baked right before serving. They make tasty and attractive appetizers.

12 large mushrooms
2 cloves garlic
1 teaspoon finely cut fresh rosemary
2 tablespoons extra virgin olive oil or butter
1/6 teaspoon sea salt
1/3 cup bread crumbs

Preheat the oven to 350 degrees. Oil a cookie sheet.

Clean the mushrooms by wiping them with a clean towel. Gently separate stems from caps.

Mince stems, garlic and rosemary.

Heat a small frying pan. Add oil, and sauté garlic and stems for 2 minutes. Add rosemary, salt and breadcrumbs. Simmer while stirring lightly for 3 minutes.

Fill each mushroom cap with 1-2 teaspoons of the mixture. Tap it down firmly. Place as much filling as will comfortably sit on the mushroom cap.

Bake for 6-8 minutes or until lightly golden and serve immediately.

SPRING BURDOCK AND NETTLES WITH CILANTRO

Freshly dug burdock and young nettle tops are a wonderful combination. Both are available in season at most health food stores. Young burdocks can be dug up as soon as their first leaves appear, and nettle tops gathered before they set flowers. When sautéed in a little dark roasted sesame oil, the strong individual flavors of burdock and nettles blend harmoniously.

2 tablespoons dark roasted sesame oil or extra virgin olive oil

2 cups burdock root, grated large or shaved

2 cups nettles, finely cut

1/4 cup water

1 tablespoon tamari soy sauce

3 tablespoons cilantro finely cut

Dandelion flowers for garnish

Heat a skillet, then add oil, and sauté burdock until they release a pleasant nutty aroma. Add nettles and sauté a little longer.

Pour water in the skillet, cover and simmer for 10-15 min.

Season with tamari soy sauce and simmer 2 minutes.

Add cilantro. Mix well and serve garnished with dandelion flowers.

ARAME SEA VEGETABLES WITH ORANGE RIND

Arame is a broad-leaf sea vegetable. The store-bought variety has been precooked, shredded thin, and dried. It brings a wonderful dark centering color to the meal that makes all the other dishes shine brighter. The method used to cook the arame is water sautéing, without oil, combined with the long-time slow-cooking technique.

1 cup dry arame, packed tightly
2 cups water
1 onion, cut in crescent moons
1 tablespoon tamari soy sauce
1 tablespoon maple syrup
1 orange, plus 1 extra slice for garnish

Soak arame in water for 10 - 20 minutes.

Heat a saucepan and sauté the onions in 1 tablespoon water.

Lift the arame out of the water with your hands and transfer on top of the onions. Any dirt will settle to the bottom. Pour the soaking water over the arame, discarding the last 4-5 tablespoons.

Bring arame and onions to a boil, and simmer covered until tender—about 20 minutes.

Drain the remaining liquid off. Season the arame with tamari and maple syrup.

Grate the orange rind and press the juice out of the orange. Add both to the arame and serve.

WILD GREEN SAUTÉ

Fresh dandelion greens can be found everywhere in the spring. Pick them before they set flowers. Look also for wild mustard greens and watercress as a substitute. By blanching wild greens first in boiling water, with a dash of salt, the extreme bitterness is drawn out and discarded with the water. Other leafy greens can be used instead but may have to cook longer.

1 quart water
1 dash sea salt
2 cups dandelion greens, loosely packed
2 tablespoons butter or extra virgin olive oil
1 tablespoon tamari soy sauce

Bring the water to a boil. Add salt.

Blanch the greens in water quickly, for 10 seconds.

Drain the greens well, and cut them in thin diagonals

Heat a frying pan, add oil, and sauté the greens for 2 minutes.

Season with tamari soy sauce and simmer for 1 minute

PRESSED NEW RADISHES

Pressing vegetables is a quick way to make a light pickle. Radishes taste less sharp after the pressing process.

1 big bunch of radishes
1 teaspoon of sea salt
1 1/2 teaspoons of vinegar

Rinse and trim the radishes. Slice into thin rounds and place in a bowl.

Mix radishes with sea salt. Place a smaller bowl on top of the radishes. Leave a heavy weight, a large rock for example, in the smaller bowl. Let them sit under pressure for 20 minutes to 2 hours.

Pour off the liquid that has been pressed out of the radishes.

Season with vinegar, mix well, and let the radishes rest for 5 minutes before serving.

LATE SPRING MENU

Barley Mushroom Soup with Scallions
Green Arugula Salad with Sweet Vinegar Miso Dressing
Oatmeal Cookies
Almond Yogurt Dessert

The homemade yogurt needs to be started the day before using it. The barley has to be soaked for 8 hours. Bake the cookies while the soup is simmering. Then make the salad and yogurt dessert.

BARLEY MUSHROOM SOUP WITH SCALLIONS

Barley is chewy, delightful in soups, and soothing for the digestive system. It is cooked in a well-flavored broth with mushrooms. If fresh shitake is not available use dried, and soak them 30 minutes before slicing them. White button mushrooms or morels can be used with, or instead of, shitake mushrooms. If desired, add lightly sautéed cubed beef, cooked beans, or fried tofu, along with the stock, and let it simmer with the barley and vegetables.

1 cup whole barley

3 cups water

1 dash vinegar or juice from cultured foods

2 tablespoons extra virgin olive oil

2 cups diced onions

1 cup fresh shitake mushrooms, cut fine

1 cup diced carrots

1/2 cup diced celery

4-6 cups vegetable stock, or nourishing stock cooked on bones (see Soups)

1-2 tablespoons sea salt

Fresh ground pepper

1 scallion cut in long thin diagonals

Rinse the barley. Add water and a dash of vinegar, or juice from cultured foods. Let soak for 8 hours.

Precook the barley for 30 minutes in the soaking water.

Heat a big heavy bottomed soup pot, add oil and sauté onions for 1 minute. Place a lid on top and simmer for 20 seconds. Add shitake, carrots and celery, and sauté for two minutes.

Pour stock and barley over the vegetables; bring to a boil and let simmer, covered for 30 minutes.

Season the soup with salt and pepper. Simmer for 5 more minutes. Serve in individual serving bowls and garnish with scallions.

GREEN ARUGULA SALAD WITH SWEET VINEGAR MISO DRESSING

Lettuce is abundant in spring as it grows best in cool weather. Arugula is now a common herb in the produce section. It has a distinctive flavor and is often served with smoked meat. The dressing is made with a delicious light miso and raw honey.

1/2 head of lettuce
1 cup arugula, cut into bite-size pieces

Rinse and dry the lettuce. Tear or cut in smaller pieces.
Mix lettuce with arugula and place in individual serving bowls.

SWEET VINEGAR MISO DRESSING

1 tablespoon white miso
1 tablespoon raw honey
1 tablespoon mustard
1/2 teaspoon sea salt
3 tablespoons water
3 tablespoons extra virgin olive oil (optional)

Mix miso, honey, mustard and sea salt well, stir in water, and lastly add oil.
Before serving, pour 1 1/2 tablespoons of dressing over each bowl of lettuce.

OATMEAL COOKIES

These old-fashioned oatmeal cookies are crisp and rich. Instead of carob use dark chocolate chips or cut dried fruit. Blend in whole oat flakes for a heartier cookie. For better digestibility, mix all the dry ingredients, except baking soda. Add one teaspoon of vinegar or liquid from cultured foods to the wet ingredients. Mix the batter and let it rest for 6 hours at room temperature. Add the baking soda to a little flour, and mix it completely into the dough before spooning the dough onto the baking sheet.

1 1/2 cups rolled quick oats
1/2 cup whole wheat pastry flour
1/2 teaspoon sea salt
1/2 cup baking soda
1 cup walnuts, chopped
1/2 cup unsweetened carob chips (optional)
1/2 cup rice syrup
3 tablespoons extra virgin olive oil or butter
1/2 cup maple syrup
1/2 cup water

Preheat the oven to 350 degrees.

In a blender grind the oats to flour.

Heat a skillet and lightly toast the oat flour.

Mix oat and pastry flours, sea salt, baking soda, walnuts and carob chips together.

Whisk rice syrup, oil and maple syrup together, and add liquids to dry ingredients. If the dough is too dry, adjust by adding water.

Spoon the dough onto an oiled baking sheet. Cookies will expand, so leave room in between. Bake the cookies for 15 minutes, then flip over and bake for another 5-10 minutes, or until light golden. Let cool before serving.

ALMOND YOGURT DESSERT

It is simple to make your own yogurt from raw milk. It should be eaten within three to five days. If you prefer the milk to be pasteurized, you can heat it to 140-160 degrees first, and then let it cool to 110 degrees. The beneficial bacteria in yogurt mature and wither quickly when sweeteners are added. To ensure healthy bacteria count, blend instead one banana with the yogurt in place of the maple syrup. For a change use vanilla instead of almond extract.

1 quart yogurt made of whole milk (see recipe below)
2 tablespoons pure almond extract
1/2 cup maple syrup
Dandelion flowers for garnish

Blend the yogurt with almond extract and maple syrup.

Pour into small individual serving glasses and garnish with dandelion flowers.

YOGURT

4 cups whole milk
1/4 cup plain unpasteurized yogurt or 5 grams yogurt starter

Heat the milk to about 110 degrees F, then transfer it to a glass bowl.

Whisk in plain yogurt. Cover the bowl with a cloth and let it sit in a warm place (around 100-110 degrees) for 6-12 hours. An oven with a pilot light works well.

When the yogurt has thickened, cool it in the refrigerator for another 6 hours.

BLOSSOMING AND MATURING— COOKING FOR SUMMER

I love the heat of summer, and the abundance of bright, colorful, sweet-scented flowers. I leap with joy and soar on the wings of summer's out-breathing. From early morning I feel the sun beckoning me to be outside and witness the wonders of the world. I feel a longing to be in the garden, swim in cool waters, and go for long walks in the fields and enchanted woods. The magical, long, warm, dusky evenings call for picnics, bonfire gatherings, and music making. I gaze for hours at summer sunsets and sparkling stars, with a deep inner feeling of being nearer the origin of life. I feel cradled in the lap of divinity.

In summer everything seems enveloped in solar warmth and vast, sustaining life forces. The air feels full of a subtle presence. As bees buzz from one flower to the next in search of nectar, I rejoice in picking edible blossoms for my summer meals. The peppery nasturtiums and blue star-shaped borage blossoms especially draw my attention. Golden blossoms of zucchini, butternut, and pumpkin decorate many-shaded green foliages. Summer squashes will be popping out soon, but winter squashes still need a long time to mature. Already the cooling cucumber, melon, and green string beans have developed pods and fruits.

I harvest broccoli, along with many fresh young, leafy greens. These leaves of kale and collards reach out to catch the attention of the sun. Summer onions, planted in early spring, bulk on top of the humus-rich soil alongside dark red and purple beets nearly bursting out of the ground. Sweet corn stalks bow gently in the wind as summer cabbages and firm white heads of cauliflower steadily grow stronger. Fields of flint corn, wheat, and oats reach into the far distance. They flower without much notice. I am touched by the modesty of these grains, knowing well that the health of humanity depends largely upon them.

 Explore

Dark summer berries, such as elderberries, wild grapes, blackberries, and black caps, have many wonderfully nourishing qualities. Look for them along the less traveled country roads. Rinse the berries and cook them in a little apple juice for 10 minutes. Strain the liquid and bottle it hot in small canning jars. This is medicine for the winter.

SUMMER MENUS

These summer menus bring a feeling of lightness and expansion. They stimulate fullness, transmit coolness, and strive to move heat to the surface. They are delicious and nourishing. Each meal is an artistic creation, rich in color, shape and character.

EARLY SUMMER MENU

Tamari Soup with Cauliflower and Lemon

Rice with Grated Carrots, Parsley, and Sunflower Seeds

Poached Cod with Lemon Paprika

New Potatoes with Dill Butter

Fried Yellow Squash Rounds

Young Summer Greens with Mustard Dressing

Carrot Flower Pickles

Sun Tea with Lemon Balm

CELEBRATION OF SUMMER MENU

Summer Spritzer

Whole Wheat Sourdough Bread with Herbed Hummus

Cucumber Rice Rolls with Dipping Sauce

Pasta Rolls with Creamy Parsley

Grilled Sweet Corn in the Husk

Summer Shish Kebab
Green Rounds with Peanut Sauce
Kefir Lemon Cooler
Sweet Sticky Blueberry Nut Bars

LATE SUMMER MENU

Cool Refreshing Lemon Dill Cucumber Soup
Golden Polenta Triangles
Spicy Kidney Beans
Colorful Brine Pickles Salad with Vinaigrette

EARLY SUMMER MENU

Tamari Soup with Cauliflower and Lemon
Rice with Grated Carrots, Parsley, and Sunflower Seeds
Poached Cod with Lemon Paprika
New Potatoes with Dill Butter
Fried Yellow Squash Rounds
Young Summer Greens with Mustard Dressing
Carrot Flower Pickles
Sun Tea with Lemon Balm

Prepare the pickled carrot flowers a day or two in advance. Soak the rice overnight. Let the tea bask in the hot sun all day. While cooking the rice, prepare the soup, potatoes, greens, and squash. Finish with the poached fish.

TAMARI SOUP WITH CAULIFLOWER AND LEMON

This soup is deliciously refreshing served at room temperature on a hot summer day. The beauty of this soup is that just one single vegetable is appreciated and enjoyed.

1 quart light sea vegetable stock (see Soups)
1-2 cups small cauliflower florets
3-4 tablespoons tamari soy sauce
4 slices of lemon

Bring the stock to a boil. Add cauliflower florets and let simmer for 3-4 minutes, depending on size. The florets should be tender and crispy.

Season with tamari soy sauce and simmer for 1 minute.

Place the hot soup in individual serving bowls with a slice of lemon in each bowl. Let the soup cool to room temperature and serve.

RICE WITH GRATED CARROTS, PARSLEY, AND SUNFLOWER SEEDS

The carrots and parsley add lightness and festive colors to the rice. The cooking method used in this recipe is very gentle and at the same time strengthening. Cooked this way the rice becomes very sweet and flavorful. It is my favorite way of cooking rice. Special pots called Ohsawa pots are made for this purpose and can be bought through catalogs. The rice can be boiled instead for 60 minutes using an additional 1 1/2 cups of water or light sea vegetable soup stock.

2 cups medium grain brown rice
2 1/2 cups water
1 teaspoon vinegar or liquid from cultured foods
1 pinch sea salt
1/2 cup carrots, grated
3 tablespoons parsley minced
1 cup fresh shelled sunflower seeds
1/2 teaspoon sea salt

Rinse and soak the rice in water with vinegar or liquid from cultured foods, in a glass, ceramic, or stainless steel bowl or pot for 4-8 hours before cooking. Make sure you have a cover or a small plate that fits. The bowl or pot must be big enough to hold the rice when it has expanded, and small enough to fit inside the pressure cooker.

Pour less than 1 inch of water in the pressure cooker. Place the bowl with rice inside the pressure cooker. Add salt and cover the bowl. Place the lid on the pressure cooker and bring the pressure up. Keep the pressure steady and cook for 40 minutes. Let the pressure come down slowly. Remove the lid of the pressure cooker.

Place the rice, with parsley and grated carrot, into a serving bowl. The hot rice will steam the carrot and parsley lightly. Cover the rice with a cotton towel or rice mat and let sit until serving.

Meanwhile, wash and drain the sunflower seeds. Heat a skillet and roast the seeds over medium heat until golden and fragrant. Sprinkle with sea salt and serve with the rice.

POACHED COD WITH LEMON PAPRIKA

Poaching is a light way of preparing fish that honors the subtle, delicious flavors. Traditionally cod was fished for in the spring, fall, and winter months. Today it is caught year-round. Cod is overfished in the Atlantic Ocean. Buy fish caught from the Pacific Ocean, or farm-raised organically. It is best to use one whole big piece of fresh fish for poaching. Occasionally I use frozen fish, as in this dish. Use fresh saltwater or freshwater fish available in your area, instead of cod.

1 1/2 pounds frozen cod
2 quarts of water
1 pinch of sea salt
2 bay leaves
1/2 teaspoon paprika
4 slices of lemon

Slowly thaw the fish in the refrigerator for 12 hours. Rinse the fish in cold water.

Bring water, salt and bay leaves to a boil. Immerge the cod in boiling water and remove the pot from heat. If the fish portion is large, place a flame-tamer between the pot and heat source to keep the water hot. It is important that the water is not boiling. Let the fish rest in the water for 7-10 minutes.

Gently transfer the fish to a serving dish. Sprinkle paprika on each slice of lemon. Decorate with lemon slices.

NEW POTATOES WITH DILL BUTTER

The first new potatoes of the year are wonderful alone, or served with butter, salt, and fresh dill.

1 pound new potatoes
2 cups water
1/2 teaspoon sea salt

8 tablespoons fresh butter (see Late Winter Menu)
2 tablespoons fresh dill cut very fine

Wash the potatoes lightly. Do not peel. Place potatoes in a pot and add water. They do not need to be totally immerged in water.

Bring water to a boil, add salt, and let simmer for 10-15 minutes, depending on size of potatoes. Use a thin needle to check when done.

Meanwhile, stir the butter with dill. Drain the potatoes, peel if necessarily, and serve hot with dill butter on the side.

FRIED YELLOW SQUASH ROUNDS

Yellow squash and zucchini are delicious in a variety of vegetable combinations, yet stand out on their own, sautéed in butter or olive oil.

2 medium yellow squash cut in thick rounds
2 tablespoon butter or extra virgin olive oil
1/4 teaspoon sea salt
1 teaspoon dried garlic powder or 1 clove garlic, minced fine

Heat a large frying pan. Add butter or oil. Fry the yellow squash rounds over medium heat. Add a pinch of salt and garlic. Turn the squash gently from time to time. They are done when tender and golden brown.

Season the squash rounds with the rest of the salt.

YOUNG SUMMER GREENS WITH MUSTARD DRESSING

In early summer a wide variety of new leafy greens are available. Use young kale, Chinese cabbage, bok choy, collards, turnip, and beet greens. Stems are tender at this time of year, so leave them on the greens.

1/2 pound of different small greens cleaned
2 quarts water

Bring two quarts water to a boil.

Immerse the whole green leaves in boiling water and blanch for 2-4 minutes.

Drain and cool the greens. Cut them first in halves along the stem, then in fine diagonals. Pour the dressing over the greens right before serving.

MUSTARD DRESSING

8 tablespoons extra virgin olive oil
3 tablespoons rice or balsamic vinegar
2 tablespoons water
1 tablespoon Dijon mustard
1 tablespoon maple syrup
1/2 teaspoon salt
1/4 teaspoon fresh oregano minced
1/4 teaspoon fresh rosemary, cut very fine

Whisk all ingredients for the dressing together in a bowl.

CARROT FLOWER PICKLES

These light carrot pickles are very decorative. They add zest and crunch to the meal. The carrot flowers become more delicious if allowed to marinate for several days. Other vegetables can be pickled the same way. Umeboshi vinegar is used in this marinade. It is the brine of fermented medicinal Japanese umeboshi plums. Sea salt and 1/4 cup whey from yogurt can be used instead of umeboshi vinegar. The pickles need to sit with a tightly fitting lid at room temperature for 3 days.

2 wide carrots
1/2 to 2/3 cup umeboshi vinegar
1 cup water

Cut the carrots into flowers by making thin wedges on the side of the carrot, in the growing direction. Then cut the carrot into thin rounds and place these "flowers" in a jar.

Mix umeboshi vinegar and water. Pour the mixture over the carrot flowers and let rest for two hours, or several days at room temperature, before serving. Use the marinade in dressings or soups.

SUN TEA WITH LEMON BALM

Sun tea is brewed by the light and warmth of the sun. It is deliciously refreshing served room temperature.

1 orange
4 herbal tea bags or 4 tablespoons dried sweet herbs
Lemon balm leaves, 1/4 cup fresh or 2 tablespoon dried
1 quart water

Peel the rind off the orange with a potato peeler.

Place herbal tea and lemon balm leaves in a 1-quart glass jar. Add water and orange rind. Cover mouth of jar with a washcloth, and let it sit in the sun for 4-8 hours.

Slice the orange. Serve sun tea in glasses decorated with orange slices and fresh lemon balm leaves.

CELEBRATION OF SUMMER MENU

Summer Spritzer

Whole Wheat Sourdough Bread with Herbed Hummus

Cucumber Rice Rolls with Dipping Sauce

Pasta Rolls with Creamy Parsley

Grilled Sweet Corn in the Husk

Summer Shish Kebab

Green Rounds with Peanut Sauce

Kefir Lemon Cooler

Sweet Sticky Blueberry Nut Bars

This simple menu is ideal for a festive get-together for 8 to 10 people. Almost all dishes are finger foods that can be prepared in advance. Make the kefir at least two days before the celebration. Make and bake the bread the day before. Soak chickpeas and nuts for 8 hours. While cooking rice and pasta, make the bars, and prepare vegetables for the remaining dishes. Assemble the rolls and make the spread, sauces, and lemon cooler. Finish the meal preparation by grilling the corn and shish kebab. Pick fresh flowers for decoration and garnishes. To clean hands before eating, pass out small, hot towels steamed over lavender water. Have an empty bowl ready for used towels.

SUMMER SPRITZER

This lovely refreshing drink is just right for a festive summer gathering.

2 oranges
2 cups boiling water
4 tea bags of herbal, black or green tea
1/2 to 1 cup raw honey
2 quarts ice-cold sparkling water

Peel the orange rind in small slivers with a potato peeler. Place tea bags and orange rind in a teapot and add boiling water.

Let the tea cool to room temperature. Add the juice of the orange and raw honey. Stir until completely diluted.

Serve in decorative glasses with small slices of orange rind in each glass.

WHOLE WHEAT SOURDOUGH BREAD

Sourdough breads are a pleasure to make and eat. Many people today need to learn how to digest this coarse, nutritious, and delicious whole wheat bread. In transitions and for parties, substitute some whole wheat with sifted unbleached white flour. The amount of flour can vary depending on types of wheat and the moisture content of the flour. If you are taking good care of the starter, it will get stronger and last a long time. In Denmark I had a mother dough that was over 100 years old, passed down though generations. Sourdough bread keeps well for 6-10 days in a cool place. Store the bread in paper placed inside a plastic bag. Week-old bread can be sliced and reheated by toasting or steaming before serving.

MOTHER DOUGH, THE STARTER

1 cup freshly ground whole wheat flour
1 cup water
6 x 1/4 cups water
6 x 1/4 cups whole wheat flour

Mix 1 cup flour and 1 cup water in a glass bowl or jar. Cover with a cotton cloth and put in a cool place or outside in a shaded area.

Every day for the next 6 days, transfer the mother dough to a new clean bowl or jar. Feed the starter with 1/4 cup water and 1/4 cup flour, cover with a cloth, and return it to the cool place.

Keep at least a cup of the mother dough starter, storing it in the refrigerator. Use a jar with a lid that allows it to breathe. If kept longer than one week, feed it again as described above, and put it back in the refrigerator.

The day before baking, feed the mother dough with enough flour and water to make 3 cups. Two cups are for the bread, and one cup is to keep for next bread-making. The mother dough is always kept separate from the bread dough, and fed whole-wheat flour and water every week.

(Whole Wheat Sourdough Bread – Continued)

SOURDOUGH BREAD

3 cups mother dough or starter
1 3/4 cups of water
1 tablespoon sea salt
4–5 cups whole wheat flour or half unbleached white flour
Butter or olive oil

Place 2 cups mother dough in a large mixing bowl. Place 1 cup in a pint-size jar in the refrigerator for the next bread-making. Add water and salt to the mother dough in the bowl. Mix well with a wooden spoon.

Add flour a little at a time. Form a firm but moist, light dough, the consistency of an ear lobe. Too much flour will make the dough hard.

Knead the dough in the bowl for 5 minutes. Cover with a moist cotton cloth and let rise in a warm place to double size, about 3 hours. The rising time may vary. Over-rising makes the bread sour.

Oil a bread pan with butter or olive oil.

Moisten hands. Knead the dough gently for a minute. Place the dough in the bread pan. The dough should fill the pan about one-half to two-thirds.

Let the dough rise again in a warm place, for 3 hours, or until doubled in size.

Heat the oven to 325 degrees and place the bread on one of the top shelves. Bake for 40-60 minutes or until golden. The bread will sound hollow when it is tapped.

Remove the bread from pan, and let cool on an oven rack before slicing.

HERBED HUMMUS

Hummus is a delicious spread from the Middle East. It is usually prepared with chickpeas and lots of fresh garlic. Other light-colored beans can be used for this spread, like navy beans and black-eyed peas. Kombu is added as a flavor enhancer and as an aid to digestion. Tahini is a paste made of freshly ground raw or roasted sesame seeds.

1 cup chickpeas cleaned, rinsed and soaked for 8 hours
3 cups water
2 inches kombu sea vegetable
1 teaspoon sea salt
1/4 cup extra virgin olive oil
1/4 cup tahini
1/4 cup fresh lemon juice
1/4 cup finely chopped parsley
1/2 cup minced fresh herbs like; rosemary, sage, anise, thyme and marjoram

Drain the beans and discard the soaking water. Place chickpeas, water and kombu in a pressure cooker. Bring to a boil and skim off any foam that arises.

Place a lid on the pot and cook beans under pressure for 50 minutes. The chickpeas can be boiled for 3-4 hours in a heavy-bottomed pot. Add water from time to time. The beans are done when completely soft.

Discard any remains of kombu. Add salt, and cook beans for 10 minutes. Drain and reserve the cooking water for soup.

Add oil, tahini and lemon juice to the beans and mash them in a food mill, food processor, or by hand with a fork. Include enough cooking liquid so the hummus is smooth and creamy, but firm. While still warm, blend parsley (reserve some for garnish) and fresh minced herbs, evenly, into the chickpeas with a spoon. Chill until ready to serve with the sourdough bread. Garnish with parsley.

**CUCUMBER RICE ROLLS WITH
DIPPING SAUCE**

Rice rolls are wonderful and satisfying. The rolls can be filled with a variety of colorful vegetables, scrambled eggs, and marinated or cooked fish. Other favorites are avocado rolls and rice rolls with shrimps.

1 medium carrot, cut in thin matchsticks
6 sheets of toasted nori sea vegetables
1 bamboo mat (sushi mat)
3 cups cooked brown rice or white sushi rice
3 tablespoons umeboshi plum paste
3 inch cucumber, seeded and cut into matchsticks
5 spring onions, cut in thin diagonals

Place the matchstick carrots in a pot with two tablespoons water. Bring to a boil and simmer for 20 seconds. Drain and cool under cold water.

Lay one sheet of nori horizontally on a bamboo mat. Place about 1/6 of the amount of rice evenly on the lower 3/4 of the sheet of nori. Spread one teaspoon umeboshi plum paste across rice about 1/3 of the way up from the bottom. Place matchstick carrots and cucumber over the paste, and sprinkle with spring onions.

Using the mat, roll nori and rice firmly around the filling. Wet the inside 1/4 nori on the top with a little water and seal the roll like an envelope. Tuck in ends. Let the roll rest on its seal. Make the rest of the rolls the same way.

Before serving, wet a sharp knife, and cut each roll into 10-12 rounds. Serve on a platter, decoratively garnished with remaining vegetable filling.

DIPPING SAUCE

6 tablespoons tamari soy sauce
7 tablespoons water
1 tablespoon mustard

Blend ingredients well, and serve in a flat serving dish next to the nori rolls.

 ## PASTA ROLLS WITH CREAMY PARSLEY

The pasta rolls are made the same way as the rice rolls. Instead of udon, use spaghetti, buckwheat noodles or fettuccini. The filling chosen for the pasta rolls is a paste; otherwise the rolls will fall apart. Tahini, also called sesame butter, is made of freshly ground sesame seeds. Vegetable or herbs can be added to the paste if desired. Umeboshi plums are fermented medicinal Japanese green plums.

3-4 quarts of water
1 package whole wheat or rice udon
4 tablespoons tahini
1 1/2 tablespoons umeboshi plum paste
1 teaspoon finely minced ginger
1/4 cup finely cut parsley
3-4 sheets of toasted nori
1 bamboo mat
Edible flowers for garnish

Boil the water, add udon, and simmer for 8 minutes. Drain noodles. Do not rinse them.

Make a filling by blending tahini, umeboshi plum paste, ginger and parsley.

Assemble, cut and serve pasta rolls in the same way as the cucumber rice rolls. Garnish with fresh edible flowers.

GRILLED SWEET CORN IN THE HUSK

The corn can be boiled in its husks. Fresh sweet corn is mouth-watering. It needs no seasonings but can be served with fresh raw butter.

6 ears of freshly picked sweet corn

Soak corn in the husks for 1 hour.

Roast corn evenly over coals of an open fire, 3-4 minutes on each side. Cook thoroughly, but don't overcook.

Leave corn in the husks and serve hot.

SUMMER SHISH KEBAB

Shish kebabs are originally a Turkish dish, made with lamb and various vegetables.
Use tempeh or tofu instead of lamb.

1-2 pound lamb or other meat in chunks
4 cloves garlic
1 cup white wine
1 teaspoon sea salt
Dashes of pepper

1 quart water
2 carrots cut in wedges
6 big broccoli florets
6 big mushrooms
3 red, yellow or green peppers, cut into rectangles
6 big rounds of yellow squash
12 small onions, peeled
12 metal or wooden skewers soaked in water

Marinate the meat in garlic, wine, sea salt and pepper.

Heat 1 quart of water and blanch all vegetables for 1 minute, except onions. Boil the onions last, for 5 minutes.

Place the vegetables on skewers decoratively.

Place the meat on separate skewers to ensure even cooking.

Place all skewers on racks in front of hot coals, or on pan under a broiler.

Broil shish kebab for 3-4 minutes. Turn, broil 3-4 minutes; turn and broil again 3-4 minutes. Serve hot.

GREEN ROUNDS WITH PEANUT SAUCE

The green roll can be filled with colorful lightly steamed vegetables and similar fillings, as suggested for the rice and pasta rolls. Decorate the serving dish with edible flowers.

2 quarts water
1 pinch salt
3 big leaves Chinese cabbage
3 big leaves collard greens
1 bamboo mat (sushi mat)

Bring the water to a boil. Add salt. Blanch the Chinese cabbage leaves for 1 minute. Blanch collard greens for 4 minutes. Immerse the leaves in cold water to stop cooking. Cut the stem off collard greens and cook for an additional 2 minutes.

Place the Chinese cabbage leaves on a bamboo mat, with the inside of leaves facing up. Position leaves so stems alternately face away from and toward you. They should overlap to fit the mat. Place collard greens the same way on top of Chinese cabbage. Place stems horizontally from left to right on the bottom third. Fold in the end of the leaves on both sides. Use the mat to roll greens around stems tightly.

Remove the mat and cut the roll into 1/2-inch rounds. Place the rounds decoratively on a serving plate.

PEANUT SAUCE

1/2 cup freshly ground peanut butter
2 tablespoons tamari soy sauce
1/2 cups water
2 tablespoons ginger juice

Stir the peanut butter with tamari soy sauce and enough water to form a thick sauce. Season the sauce with ginger juice.

KEFIR LEMON COOLER

This refreshing cooler is a common Scandinavian summer dessert. It is served with small sweet cookies. The kefir grains can be bought through a mail order catalog (see Resources) or obtained from a friend making kefir. A powdered kefir starter is available at health food stores and can be used instead of the kefir grains.

1 quart kefir
2 lemons
1/4 – 1/2 cup maple syrup
2 tablespoons quick oat flakes (optional)

Grate the rind of the lemons finely. Cut the lemons in slices.

In a blender, grind oat flakes into flour.

Whisk flour, lemon rind and maple syrup into kefir. Let it sit for several hours.

Pour into decorative glasses and garnish with lemon slices.

HOMEMADE KEFIR

1 quart raw whole milk
1/6 cup kefir grains

Place kefir grains in a glass jar. Pour the milk into the jar and cover with a cotton cloth. Let it sit at room temperature for 12-24 hours, depending on desired flavor (the longer it sits, the more sour the flavor).

Strain the grains from the kefir with a nylon strainer. Pour a little fresh milk over the grains and store in the refrigerator until ready to make another batch.

Keep homemade kefir in a glass jar in the refrigerator. It will stay fresh at least two weeks.

SWEET STICKY BLUEBERRY NUT BARS

These bars can be made with different seasonal berries. The berries add tartness to the sweet bars. Use pecans instead of walnuts. Try making individual little cakes instead of bars, using muffin pans (this recipe yields 18). For better digestibility, mix everything except the baking powder. Let the batter rest for 6 hours in room temperature. Add the baking powder to a little flour, and mix it completely into the dough, then continue as described.

2 cups and 1/2 cup whole wheat pastry flour
1/2 teaspoon sea salt
1/2 teaspoon baking powder (optional)
1 cup walnuts, soaked in lightly salted water for 6 hours
1/2 cup extra virgin olive oil
1/2 cup maple syrup
1 teaspoon vinegar or liquid from cultured food
2 eggs
2 tablespoons vanilla extract
2 cups rice syrup
2 cups blueberries

Preheat the oven to 350 degrees.

In a bowl mix two cups flour, sea salt, baking powder and nuts.

Mix oil, maple syrup and vinegar. Add wet ingredients to the flour. Make dough, and form into a ball.

Pat the dough evenly into a lightly greased baking pan 9 x 13 inches. Bake 15 minutes, or until light golden and firm. Remove from oven and set aside.

Meanwhile, whisk together eggs, vanilla extract, 1/2 cup flour and rice syrup.

Pour mixture over crust. Place berries on top and return the pan to oven. Bake 15-20 minutes or until top is lightly browned.

Cool and cut into squares. Place on a serving tray.

LATE SUMMER MENU

Cool Refreshing Lemon Dill Cucumber Soup
Golden Polenta Triangles
Spicy Kidney Beans
Colorful Brine Pickles Salad with Vinaigrette

Make the brine pickles several days in advance. I make these pickles throughout the summer, so I have a jar ready at all times in the refrigerator. The night before serving this meal, rinse and soak the beans. Grind, roast, and soak the corn flour as well. The following day cook the beans and polenta. While the beans and grains are cooking, prepare the soup and salad.

COOL REFRESHING LEMON DILL CUCUMBER SOUP

The cucumber soup is smooth, cooling, and rich in flavor. I find it most satisfying puréed. It can be strained for a bisque-like soup. This cucumber soup is wonderful on a hot summer day. I like to serve it at a temperature slightly warmer than refrigeration. Lemon and dill add a complementary garnish.

2-3 medium cucumbers, peeled and diced small
1 small red onion, diced finely
1 stalk celery, diced finely
2 tablespoons fresh dill, finely cut
1 cup water
1 tablespoon grated lemon rind
Juice of 1/2 to 1 lemon
1 to 1 1/2 teaspoons sea salt
1 cup homemade kefir or yogurt (optional)
Sprigs of fresh dill
Thin decorative slices of lemon and cucumber for garnish

Place the cucumber, onion, celery, dill and water in a food blender or food processor. Puree until smooth. Season the soup with lemon rind, lemon juice and sea salt.

Blend the yogurt or kefir well into the soup.

Served immediately, or let the flavors blend in the refrigerator for several hours first. Mix well before serving. Garnish each bowl with fresh sprigs of dill and slices of lemon and cucumber.

GOLDEN POLENTA TRIANGLES

In traditional American Indian cooking, whole corn is cooked with lime or wood ash until the hulls have loosened and the corn is soft. The corn is rinsed and cooked again before it is ground into dough. This dough, called masa, is used especially for tortillas. In this dish corn is milled, roasted, then soaked in a rich broth, and boiled until soft and smooth. If the weather is very hot, soak the cornmeal in the refrigerator, or use water with an added dash of vinegar, instead of soup stock.

1 cup corn flour or meal
2 1/2 cups nourishing stock, cooked from bones
1/4 teaspoon sea salt
1/2 to 1 cup extra virgin olive oil or butter for frying (optional)

Roast the freshly ground corn flour lightly, in a heavy bottom pan, by stirring until a delightful aroma is released, and the flour is slightly golden.

When the flour has cooled, place it in a heavy-bottomed stainless steel pot. Add the soup stock. Let the cornmeal soak 8 hours in a cool place.

Add sea salt and bring the corn mixture to a boil, stirring regularly to avoid sticking. Place a flame spreader under the pot and cook covered over low heat for 30-40 minutes, stirring occasionally.

Rinse a glass bread pan in cold water. Pour the cooked cornmeal, or polenta, into the pan and let cool completely.

Transfer polenta to a cutting board. Cut the polenta into thick slices then on the diagonal, to create triangles. Serve polenta triangles at room temperature with hot beans, or fry the triangles before serving.

SPICY KIDNEY BEANS

This spicy hot bean dish brings body heat to the surface. The strength of the spices varies with their quality. If they are old, they are less pungent.

1 cup kidney beans, cleaned, rinsed and soaked 8 hours
3 cups cold water
3-inch piece of kombu sea vegetable
4 tablespoons olive oil
1/4 teaspoon oregano
1/4 teaspoon cumin
1/4 teaspoon crushed red chili pepper or a pinch of cayenne.
1 onion, diced small
1/2 stalk celery, diced small
2 tablespoons tamari soy sauce
2 tablespoons fine cut parsley for garnish

Drain beans and discard soaking water. Place the beans in a pot or pressure cooker. Add water. Bring to a rapid boil and skim off any foam that arises. Add kombu and place the lid on the pot or pressure cooker. If boiling the beans, let them simmer until completely soft. This may take 3-4 hours. Add water whenever necessary. Otherwise, pressure cook beans for one hour over very low heat. Turn off heat and let pressure come down slowly, on its own. Discard remains of kombu.

Meanwhile, heat a big skillet. Add oil, and sauté spices and herbs quickly, then add onions and sauté for 2 minutes. Place lid on skillet and simmer for 20 seconds. Add celery and sauté a few minutes, before adding beans and enough cooking liquid for the bean dish to be saucy. Let it all simmer for 10 minutes.

Season the beans with tamari soy sauce. The spicy kidney bean dish is served over the polenta triangles. Garnish with parsley.

COLORFUL BRINE PICKLES SALAD
WITH VINAIGRETTE

These pickles are wonderful and easy to make throughout the year. It is a little tricky to ferment in the summer when room temperature is higher than the preferred 72 degrees. Either place pickles in a cool place, for example in the basement, or use umeboshi plums instead of salt, as in this recipe. Umeboshi plums are fermented Japanese medicinal green plums. A quarter cup of whey may be added to the water as a starter for the fermentation process.

3 cups broccoli florets, carrots rounds or flowers, or cauliflower florets

1 cup red onion cut into crescent moons

2 cloves garlic, sliced

1 tablespoon dill seeds

3/4 quart water, boiled and cooled

1 umeboshi plum or 1 tablespoon sea salt

1 big head of lettuce, washed and cut in diagonal

1/3 cup extra virgin olive oil

1/4 cup balsamic vinegar

Sea salt and pepper to taste

Place the vegetables, garlic, and dill seeds in a quart glass jar.

Purée the umeboshi plum or dilute the salt in a little water, and add to the jar. Fill the jar with water. Cover jar with a tight-fitting lid.

Let the jar sit in a dark room, preferably less than 72 degrees, for 2-3 days. If pickling in cool weather 5-7 days might be needed. The vegetables will be firm, crisp, and have a delicious unique flavor.

Whisk the oil and vinegar together. Season the vinaigrette with salt and pepper. Serve a small assortment of brine pickles for each person on a bed of lettuce with the dressing.

DRAWING IN—
COOKING FOR AUTUMN

While the summer days are fading, autumn enters slowly with her mellower and more subdued moods. Cooler air visits from the north, while dense morning fogs cover the meadows. As the sun withdraws toward its winter home in the south, I feel my inner light stirring, calling up forces of strength and courage.

Toward the end of this season, the foliage—light green in spring, deep dark green in summer—suddenly transforms into golden, orange, and flaming crimson reds. The playful autumn winds whirl these glowing leaves around before dropping them to the ground. Piled on top of each other they create a colorful blanket to cover and protect the life beneath. The trees, getting ready for a deep winter rest, stand majestic and strong as they let go of what is needed no longer. Their bare branches reach to the lowering golden sun. Each branch, holding buds containing every tiny leaf for next year's growth, assures me that there is no end without a new beginning.

In my garden every little plant quietly withers and decays, while the seeding activity reaches its highest. As I gather seeds in separate little paper bags, I admire their unique characters and shapes. Each seed in my hand awakens faith, hope, and anticipation for what will develop and come to maturity in the coming year.

After the first light frost, I collect the last vegetables from the garden. There is emerald green broccoli and golden winter squash in abundance. Bright carrots are brought to the cellar in boxes. Winter radishes, squash, celeriac, parsnips, and ruta-baga, each in separate piles, wait patiently to be bagged. Although leeks, kale, collard greens, and brussels sprouts will keep well for another month in the fall garden, I bring some, still attached to their stalks, to the root cellar.

 Explore

Gather fresh dandelion leaves. Dig up dandelion or burdock roots. Cut leaves and roots fine. Place them loosely in a quart glass jar. Add fresh herbs such as tarragon, oregano, lemon balm and thyme. Pour naturally fermented pasteurized vinegar over the plant matter. Cover the jar with a plastic lid. Let it sit at room temperature for at least 2 weeks. Enjoy the vinegars and savor the rinsed pickled roots.

Before going to pick fall apples and pears, I stop to listen. In the distance I hear farmers baling corn for winter. For weeks different grains have been harvested, filling storage bins to the brim. Gratitude fills me for what has led to this culmination of growth. All these gifts from nature will nourish and sustain us throughout the long winter. It calls for a celebration, a feast of Thanksgiving.

AUTUMN MENUS

These autumn menus gather in the forces to bring strength and vitality. The foods and cooking styles stimulate warmth and strive to move the heat down and in. The dishes are rich, tasty, and nourishing and inspire clear thinking. Each meal is artistically arranged. Like a painting, it holds depth and strength, beautifully harmonized with light and freshness.

EARLY AUTUMN MENU

Zesty Fish Soup with Scallions

Golden Rice Pilaf

Steamed Tender Leeks with Parsley Butter

Boiled Crunchy Salad with Goddess Dressing

Grilled Caraway Beets and Red Onions

Juicy Sauerkraut

Baked Cinnamon Apples

CELEBRATION OF AUTUMN MENU

Kvass Autumn Refresher

Stuffed Herbed Buttercup Squash

Roasted Maple Turkey

Zucchini Corn Muffins with Olive Basil Dip

Fried Crispy Tempeh
Green Beans with Butter and Garlic
Collard Greens with Orange Dressing
Holiday Root Medley with Rosemary
Spiced Cranberry Chutney
Tamari Pickled Onions

LATE AUTUMN MENU

Cumin Lentil Stew with Lemon Balm
Millet Squash Pie with Parsley and Roasted Walnuts
Baked Hiziki Rolls with Orange Rind
Dark Green Kale with Creamy Dill Dressing
Radish Chrysanthemums
Danish Apple Delight

EARLY AUTUMN MENU

Zesty Fish Soup with Scallions

Golden Rice Pilaf

Steamed Tender Leeks with Parsley Butter

Boiled Crunchy Salad with Goddess Dressing

Grilled Caraway Beets and Red Onions

Juicy Sauerkraut

Baked Cinnamon Apples

It takes about two weeks to make sauerkraut. After roasting the rice, soak it overnight. Soak the walnuts for 6–8 hours. If you do not have a fish stock made, begin the preparations with that. While the rice is cooking, wash and cut the vegetables. Then grill the beets and onions, steam the leeks, simmer the soup, and boil the vegetables for the salad. Let the apples bake while everyone is eating.

ZESTY FISH SOUP WITH SCALLIONS

Bouillabaisses or fish soups are made from the catches of the day. This delicious fish soup is made from a broth cooked of fish bones, skins, and heads. I buy whole fish, fillet them, and cook a stock of the remains. The zesty flavors of ginger help move the earthiness of the soup. The soup is seasoned with umeboshi vinegar, the brine of the fermented Japanese umeboshi plums. Umeboshi vinegar gives the soup a distinct flavor that harmonizes with the ginger and garlic. As an alternative to umeboshi vinegar, season the soup with sea salt and pepper.

1 lemon

1/2 quart nourishing stock cooked from fish bones, or light sea vegetable stock

1 quart water

1/2 cup small pasta or 1 cup cooked rice

2 cloves garlic minced

1 lb. unshelled large shrimp

3/4 pound white meat fish fillets

1 inch ginger root

6 tablespoons umeboshi vinegar

4 scallions cut in thin long diagonals for garnish

Cut small pieces off lemon rind, or peel it with a potato peeler. Slice and quarter the remaining lemon.

Bring fish stock, water, pasta or rice, garlic and lemon peel to a boil. Simmer for 5 minutes. Add shrimp and fish, and simmer for 5-7 minutes. With a fork, gently separate fish into bite size pieces.

Grate the ginger and squeeze out one-tablespoon juice.

Carefully, without mashing the fish, season with ginger, umeboshi vinegar and ginger juice.

Ladle into individual serving soup dishes. Garnish with lemon quarters and scallions.

GOLDEN RICE PILAF

Whole grains are gently flavored when mixed with beans or vegetables. On a colder day, add the vegetables to the rice before cooking them. For warmer days, or a lighter dish, blanch the vegetables first for a few minutes, and blend them with the rice before serving.

2 cups short grain brown rice

4 cups water or soup stock

1 pinch sea salt

1 teaspoon turmeric

1/2 cup red pepper diced

1 teaspoon vinegar

1 cup green beans, or other firm vegetables, cut in small rounds

1/2 cup pumpkin seeds

1 tablespoon tamari soy sauce

1/4 cup black olives, pitted and sliced thinly for garnish

Rinse and drain the rice. Heat a thick-bottomed pot. Dry-roast the rice, stirring constantly, until golden.

Pour water into the pot a little at a time. Add salt, turmeric, red pepper, vinegar and green beans. Bring water slowly to a boil, place a flame tamer between the pot and the heat source and simmer covered for 45 minutes.

Heat a skillet. Rinse and drain pumpkin seeds. Dry-roast seeds until they pop and expand. Transfer to a bowl. While the seeds are still hot, sprinkle with tamari soy sauce.

Ladle the rice pilaf into a bowl. Garnish with olives and pumpkin seeds.

STEAMED TENDER LEEKS WITH PARSLEY BUTTER

When leeks are fresh and cooked well, they almost melt on the tongue. Use only the whitest part of the leek for this dish. Instead of butter use olive oil mixed with sea salt and parsley.

8 small or medium leeks, cleaned well and trimmed
Water for steaming
4 tablespoons fresh butter (see Late Winter Menu)
2 tablespoons finely chopped parsley

Cut leek stalk in 2- to 3-inch sticks.

Bring 1 inch water to a boil in a big pot. Insert a steamer and place leeks on top. Steam the leeks for 15 minutes, or until tender and soft, and transfer to a serving dish.

Stir the butter with parsley, place it on the leeks while hot, and serve.

BOILED CRUNCHY SALAD WITH GODDESS DRESSING

Blanching various fall garden vegetables makes a lovely and colorful, crunchy and digestible salad. The dressing is light, creamy, and has a nutty flavor. It uses tahini, a paste made of freshly ground raw or roasted sesame seeds. Instead of tahini try 1/2 cup freshly made yogurt.

2 quarts water
1/4 pound collard greens
2 Chinese cabbage leaves
1 cup cauliflower florets
1 cup carrot flowers
1/2 cup bunch onions cut in 1 inch pieces

Bring 2 quarts of water to a boil.

Blanch vegetables for 2-7 minutes, beginning with cauliflower, carrots, Chinese cabbage, collard greens and lastly, the bunch onions. Run cold water over vegetables to stop cooking, drain well.

Cut stems off collard leaves and discard. Cut Chinese cabbage and collard greens into thin diagonals. Mix all vegetables in a bowl.

GODDESS DRESSING

1/4 cup extra virgin olive oil
1/2 cup fresh ground tahini
1/4 cup vinegar
1/2 cup water
1 tablespoon maple syrup
1 teaspoon sea salt

Combine olive oil, tahini and vinegar. Add water and mix. Season dressing with maple syrup and salt. Pour dressing over the boiled salad and serve.

GRILLED CARAWAY BEETS AND RED ONIONS

Caraway, cumin seeds, cardamom, or cloves complement the sweet and tender beets. Other root vegetables and yellow onions can be grilled with the beets. Double the recipe and make a sweet beet soup the next day.

1 big beet
2 big red onions
4 tablespoons extra virgin olive oil
1/2 teaspoon sea salt
1 tablespoon caraway seeds
Anise leaves or lemon balm for garnish (optional)

Preheat the oven to 350 degrees.

Peel beets and onions. Cut into 1/2 inch rounds. Place onto an oiled baking sheet that fits under the grill. You may have to grill one half and then the other, depending on the size of your grill. Drizzle the oil and sprinkle salt over the beets and onions. Sprinkle caraway seeds over beets only.

Grill the beets and onions for 10-15 minutes. Turn and grill for 5-10 minutes or until soft on the inside. Garnish with anise leaves or lemon balm and serve hot.

JUICY SAUERKRAUT

I make sauerkraut regularly in fall, winter and spring. The first autumn cabbages are juicy and crisp. In the winter I sometimes have to add water to the brine of the sauerkraut, because the cabbages are very dry. Red cabbage makes beautiful sauerkraut. I like to add caraway seeds or juniper berries to the kraut as it ferments. In warm weather I double the amount of salt. The fermentation process can take longer then. A half-cup of whey may be added as a starter but is not necessarily.

6 pounds green cabbage
3 tablespoons sea salt

Take the outer layers of the cabbage and discard. Shred cabbage very fine.

With clean hands, rub salt into cabbage until it gets shiny and juicy.

Clean a one-gallon ceramic crock. Sterilize it with boiling water for 5 minutes. Pour off the water.

Pack the crock with cabbage. Press it down firmly. Place a sterilized weight, such as an upside-down plate with a rock, on top of the cabbage. After one day check if the liquid is above the plate and that no cabbage is exposed to air. Adjust the weight, or add extra brine if necessary. Boil 1/2 quart water and add one teaspoon sea salt to make brine. Let brine cool before pouring it into the jar.

Cover the jar with a kitchen towel and let sit in a dark place at room temperature, or 72 degrees, for the first 2 days. Place the crock in a cooler place, about 65 degrees, and let kraut sit for 5-12 days. Check from time to time to make sure the liquid is above the plate, but do not disturb the cabbage. When the sauerkraut is done, it has an appetizing sweet and sour taste, with a unique aroma.

Transfer the sauerkraut to smaller jars. Keep the sauerkraut in the refrigerator for months.

BAKED CINNAMON APPLES

Cinnamon and apples go well together in this warming and relaxing dessert, suited for fall. Use a variety of apples and discover how they differ in sweetness and crunch.

3 tablespoons walnuts
4 apples
1 tablespoon light miso
2 tablespoons freshly ground peanut butter (optional)
2 tablespoons water
1 tablespoon cinnamon

Soak the walnuts in lightly salted water 4-6 hours. Drain and chop them fine.

Preheat the oven to 375 degrees.

Core the apples with an apple corer or spoon. Make sure not to cut all the way through the apple.

In a small bowl mix the miso and peanut butter. Add water, cinnamon and chopped walnuts.

Spoon 1 tablespoon of the filling into each apple.

Place the apples in a baking dish. Bake in the oven for 15-20 minutes or until soft.

CELEBRATION OF AUTUMN MENU

Kvass Autumn Refresher

Stuffed Herbed Buttercup Squash

Roasted Maple Turkey

Zucchini Corn Muffins with Olive Basil Dip

Fried Crispy Tempeh

Green Beans with Butter and Garlic

Collard Greens with Orange Dressing

Holiday Root Medley with Rosemary

Spicy Cranberry Chutney

Tamari Pickled Onions

Invite friends for this meal. There is plenty for 8 to 12 people to taste a little of everything. The kvass for the autumn refresher is made weeks in advance. The pickled onions are best if allowed several days to mature but can be done in 1/2 hour. Soak the rice and walnuts separately 6 to 8 hours. Make the stuffing for the squash. Bake the squash, turkey, and zucchini muffins. Proceed by preparing the tempeh and the rest of the vegetable dishes, dressings, and sauces.

KVASS AUTUMN REFRESHER

Begin the celebration with an autumn refresher that has zest and body. It is made with kvass, a traditional Scandinavian and Russian fermented drink. The kvass needs 5-10 days to ferment, so plan ahead. Kvass is delicious as it is, sweet and slightly sour. Triple the recipe and use a gallon jar instead. The kvass stores in the refrigerator for weeks. Experiment with adding different herbs to the kvass during the fermentation process, such as thyme, rosemary, and small amounts of ginger.

1 quart water
1/4 apple, sliced
1 thick slice sourdough bread, cubed and dried completely
1 tablespoon sauerkraut
5 raisins

Place the bread and water in a pot. Bring it to a boil. Let it cool before adding it to a 1 1/2-quart size jar. Add apple, raisins, sauerkraut, and more water if necessary to fill the jar. Seal the jar with a tight-fitting lid.

Cover the jar with a towel and let it sit at room temperature for 5-10 days. If the weather is warmer, the kvass will be ready sooner. The finished kvass is a little fizzy and has a sweet and slightly sour taste.

Pour the kvass through a strainer. Discard the bread mixture and store the kvass in the refrigerator.

Serve in decorative wine glasses.

STUFFED HERBED BUTTERCUP SQUASH

Buttercup squash and other round, hard, winter squash are best to use for this dish. If you use store-bought seasoned bread stuffing, follow the directions on the package and omit everything for the dressing except the oil, celery and onions.

1 cup walnut

1 large buttercup squash

6 tablespoons extra virgin olive oil or butter

3 large onions, cubed

3 celery stalks, cubed

1/2 teaspoon sea salt

1 tablespoon dried and crushed basil

1 tablespoon dried and crushed thyme

1 tablespoon dried and crushed oregano

10 slices whole wheat sourdough bread, cut into 1/2-inch cubes

1 cup water or soup stock (see Soups) of your choice

Soak the walnuts in water for 6-8 hours. Drain and chop the nuts fine.
Preheat the oven to 350 degrees.

Wash the squash. Cut a lid off the top of the squash and scoop out seeds.

Heat a large pot and add oil or butter. Sauté onions and celery over medium heat for three minutes, then add salt and herbs, and sauté for three minutes. Mix bread and chopped nuts into vegetable mixture. Add water or stock while gently blending it all together.

Place stuffing loosely in the squash. Put the lid back on. Add the rest of the stuffing to a baking dish and cover.

Bake the squash and stuffing. The stuffing in the baking dish will be done after 30-40 minutes and the squash in 1-1 1/2 hours. Time it so both are done at the same time. Baking time depends on the size of the dish and the squash. Stick a long needle into the middle of the stuffing, pull out quickly and feel if the middle is hot.

Take both out of the oven and let sit for 15 minutes before serving.

ROASTED MAPLE TURKEY

If the turkey is frozen, thaw it slowly in the refrigerator for several days. The roasted turkey is deliciously crisp, juicy, and simple to make. It is cooked in an oven bag to secure the flavors and moisture. Serve any liquid remaining in the bag diluted with water, seasoned with salt, and thickened with just a little cornstarch for a sauce.

1 medium-size turkey
1 teaspoon sea salt
Juice of 1 lemon
8 tablespoons maple syrup
4 tablespoons extra virgin olive oil
2-3 apples, cored and cut in chunks
1 cup prunes, soaked in water
1 tablespoon flour

Preheat the oven to 400 degrees.

Rinse and dry the turkey well. Rub sea salt into the turkey, then lemon juice and maple syrup, and finish with the oil. Fill the turkey with apples and prunes.

Place the bird in an oven bag for baking, shake one tablespoon flour inside the bag, seal and cut a few holes in the top. Bake the turkey for 1 1/2 to 2 hours. Use a meat thermometer to determine if the meat is cooked all the way through. Cut the bag open and bake for another 15 minutes.

Let the turkey rest for 15 minutes before carving it. Place the pieces decoratively on a plate.

ZUCCHINI CORN MUFFINS WITH OLIVE BASIL DIP

The olive basil dip is delicious as a dipping sauce for any bread. To make the corn flour more digestible, mix the dry ingredients, except the baking soda, with the wet ingredients and let rest for 6 hours. Mix the baking powder with a little flour before adding it to the dough right before baking the muffins.

1 1/2 cups blue or yellow corn flour

1 1/2 cups of whole-wheat pastry flour

1 teaspoon sea salt

1/4 teaspoon baking soda

1 egg

3 tablespoons butter or extra virgin olive oil

1 cup water

1/2 cup apple cider or juice

1 tablespoon apple cider vinegar

2 cups grated zucchini

1/2 cup extra virgin olive oil

1 teaspoon sea salt

1/4 cup finely minced basil

Preheat the oven to 400 degrees.

Oil a muffin pan for 12.

In a large bowl mix corn flour, pastry flour, sea salt and baking soda.

In another bowl whisk together egg, butter or oil, water, apple cider and cider vinegar. Pour liquid ingredients into flour mixture and mix well. Quickly stir in the zucchini.

Pour batter into muffin pan and bake for 20-30 minutes or until golden brown. Cool on a rack for 10 minutes.

Mix olive oil, salt and minced basil. Serve in a flat dish as dipping sauce for the muffins.

FRIED CRISPY TEMPEH

Tempeh is a fermented soybean product. I make it fresh at home. (See Resources for tempeh starter and recipes.) Tempeh is very nourishing and tasty and readily available in health food stores. Fry the tempeh in two batches if necessary. The fried tempeh is seasoned with umeboshi vinegar—the brine of the fermented Japanese umeboshi plums. The umeboshi vinegar adds a tasty, sour, salty flavor to the crispy tempeh. Use instead of umeboshi vinegar 2 tablespoons apple cider vinegar and 1 teaspoon salt or 4 tablespoons tamari soy sauce.

1 1/2 pound tempeh, cubed
1/4 cup extra virgin olive oil or fresh butter
4-6 tablespoons umeboshi vinegar

Heat a skillet, add the oil or butter and fry the tempeh over medium heat until golden about 4-5 minutes. Make sure the heat is not too low or too high. Turn and fry the other side for 5 minutes.

Turn off the heat and sprinkle with umeboshi vinegar while still hot. Serve warm or room temperature.

GREEN BEANS WITH BUTTER AND GARLIC

Seasoned with butter and garlic, the green beans complement the meal well. Use extra virgin olive oil instead of butter.

2 cups green string beans, trimmed and cut in long thin diagonals
1/4 cup water
1/4 teaspoon sea salt
2 tablespoons butter
1 teaspoon garlic granulate or 1 clove fresh garlic, minced

Place the beans in a skillet with the water and simmer for 3-5 minutes. Uncover the skillet and let the green beans cook until all liquid has evaporated.

Season the beans with salt, butter and garlic. Simmer for 1 minute. The beans are done when they have a bright dark green color, are tender, but not overcooked.

COLLARD GREENS WITH ORANGE DRESSING

Collard greens taste delicious when steam boiled. It brings a sweetness and roundness to the tougher autumn greens. If the collard greens are very bitter, boil them whole in a quart of water and then cut into diagonals.

1/2 to 1 pound collard greens, finely cut on diagonal

Place the greens in a pot with 1/2 inch water. Bring the water to a boil. Turn down the heat and steam boil the greens for 5-30 minutes. Shorter time if the collard greens are to be tender, but still crisp, and longer cooking time for a nourishing, buttery soft and warming dish.

Serve with the orange dressing.

ORANGE DRESSING

1 cup orange juice
1 tablespoon grated orange rind
5 tablespoons apple cider vinegar
4 tablespoons extra virgin olive oil
1 teaspoon sea salt

In a bowl whisk all ingredients together. Let the dressing sit for 1/2 hour. Before serving whisk it again.

HOLIDAY ROOT MEDLEY WITH ROSEMARY

Cook this holiday root medley over medium heat. If the heat is too low the vegetables will be mushy. Season the dish at the end of the cooking time.

2 tablespoons extra virgin olive oil
1 cup carrots
1 cup turnips or celeriac
1 cup parsnip
2 pinches sea salt
2 tablespoons rosemary
1-2 tablespoons water
1 teaspoon sea salt

Clean the vegetables and cut into very chunky matchsticks.

Heat a frying pan. Add oil and vegetables. Sauté over medium heat for 3 minutes. Add a few pinches of salt and rosemary, cover pan and continue to cook until vegetables are done. Turn vegetables occasionally. If the vegetables get too dry add a couple of tablespoons of water.

Season the root vegetables with salt, cover the pan and continue to cook for 1 minute.

SPICED CRANBERRY CHUTNEY

This dish offers a bittersweet flavor, a bright red color, and zesty warming spices to the meal.

2 cups cranberries
1 cup apple juice
1/2 cup diced apples
5 dried apricots, cut in quarters
1/8 teaspoon sea salt
1 teaspoon cinnamon
1/2 teaspoon cloves
1/4 teaspoon allspice
1 teaspoon fresh grated ginger juice

Clean and rinse cranberries. Place them in a saucepan. Add apple juice, apples, apricots and salt. Bring to a boil and let simmer for 10 minutes.

Season the cranberries with cinnamon, cloves and allspice. Let simmer for 5 minutes.

Add the ginger juice, mix well, and serve hot.

TAMARI PICKLED ONIONS

Many firm vegetables can be pickled using this method. If they are cut thin a light pickle can be done in hours. The longer the vegetables pickle, the stronger they get. Use the brine afterwards as seasoning in soups.

2 cups loosely packed red onions, cut in crescent moons
3/4 cup unpasteurized tamari soy sauce
3/4 cup water
3 tablespoons vinegar

Place the onions in a pint jar.

Mix tamari soy sauce, water and vinegar and pour over the onions. Let the onions pickle for 1/2 hour at room temperature, or weeks in the refrigerator.

One tablespoon of pickled onions is one serving.

LATE AUTUMN MENU

Cumin Lentil Stew with Lemon Balm
Millet Squash Pie with Parsley and Roasted Walnuts
Baked Hiziki Roll with Orange Rind
Dark Green Kale with Creamy Dill Dressing
Radish Chrysanthemums
Danish Apple Delight

Soak the lentils and walnuts separately for 8 hours. Boil the millet and prepare the radishes. Make the dough for the hiziki roll and let it rest for several hours. While cooking the soup, hiziki and squash, prepare the dessert and roast the walnuts. Then assemble the millet pie and make and bake the hiziki roll. Prepare the dressing, season the soup, and boil the kale. Finish the meal by unfolding the radish flowers.

CUMIN LENTIL STEW WITH LEMON BALM

The lentil soup blends many different subtle flavors, none of them overpowering the others. Use grated lemon rind instead of lemon balm.

1 cup green lentils
4 cups water and 3 inch kombu or soup stock (see Soups)
2 bay leaves
3 cups diced onion, celery and carrot
2 tablespoons butter or extra virgin olive oil
1 tablespoon whole cumin
1 medium clove garlic, minced
1 tablespoon maple syrup
1 tablespoon barley miso
1 tablespoon tamari soy sauce
1 dash cayenne
1 carrot, cut into flowers
Lemon balm leaves

Place the lentils in a soup pot with 4 cups of water or soup stock. Bring to a boil. Skim off foam that rises to the surface. Add kombu if using water instead of soup stock and bay leaves. Cover the pot and simmer for 1-2 hours, or until lentils are completely soft. Stir from time to time. Discard any remains of kombu and remove bay leaves.

Heat the oil and sauté the cumin seeds for 10 seconds until brown.

Add vegetables, cumin and garlic to the lentils. Simmer for 10-15 minutes. Add more water if necessary.

Season the lentils with maple syrup, miso and tamari. Add a dash of cayenne.

In a little saucepan bring 1/4 cup water to a boil. Blanch the carrot flowers for 1 minute.

Serve in individual serving bowls garnished with carrot flowers and lemon balm leaves.

MILLET SQUASH PIE WITH PARSLEY AND ROASTED WALNUTS

Millet squash pie is a beautiful, sweet and nourishing dish. This recipe uses a method to cook millet which lets the grains expand slowly without getting mushy. Enhance the flavor by dry-roasting the millet in a skillet for 6-8 minutes, or until golden brown, before cooking it.

1/2 cup walnuts

5 cups water or soup stock

2 cups millet

1 dash sea salt

1 teaspoon vinegar

4 cups butternut or buttercup squash, peeled and cut in chunks

2 cups water

1/4 teaspoon sea salt

2 tablespoons parsley, cut fine

Soak the walnuts in lightly salted water 8 hours.

Bring water or stock to a boil, then add millet, salt and 1 teaspoon vinegar. Cover the pot and let it simmer for 5 minutes. Wrap the pot in a towel, then in a blanket. Let millet rest in the blanket for 3-4 hours. While still warm, pat the millet into a 9 x 9 baking dish.

Meanwhile, place the squash in a pot with one cup water and salt. Simmer covered for 20 minutes.

Puree the squash. Pour it over the millet and even it out with a spatula. Let it cool completely.

Drain the nuts and place them in the oven for 10-15 minutes at 300-325 degrees. Chop them fine.

Cut the millet pie into rectangles or squares. Garnish with parsley and roasted nuts.

BAKED HIZIKI ROLLS WITH ORANGE RIND

To serve the hiziki roll, cut it into small rounds. The decorative spiraling dough and black sea vegetables make a tasty, crisp dish that accentuates the deep orange squash pie. Tahini, a paste of freshly ground raw or roasted sesame seed, rounds and blends the flavors.

2 cups whole wheat flour

1/2 teaspoon sea salt

3 tablespoons cold pressed extra virgin olive oil

1/2 cup cold water

1 teaspoon vinegar or juice from cultured vegetables

1/2 cup dried hiziki

2-3 cups water

1 tablespoon tamari soy sauce

1-2 tablespoons grated orange rind

2 tablespoons tahini

Mix flour and salt. Combine oil, water and one teaspoon vinegar. Add mixture little by little to the flour to form dough. Gather dough in a ball, wrap in a plastic bag, and let sit in a cool place for several hours or overnight.

Soak the hiziki in water about 20 minutes. With clean hands, transfer the hiziki to a cooking pot. Pour over the soaking water but discard the last 1/4 cup with settlements. Bring the hiziki to a boil, cover and simmer for 20 minutes or until soft and tender. Pour off any remaining liquid before seasoning with tamari soy sauce, orange rind and tahini.

Preheat the oven to 350 degrees.

Dust a dry surface with flour. Roll the dough into a thin rectangular shape. Place the hiziki mixture evenly on bottom 3/4 of the dough. Roll the dough firmly around the hiziki. Close off ends. Use a fork to prick holes on top of the roll.

Place the roll on an oiled baking sheet and bake for 40 minutes or until golden brown. Let the hiziki roll cool before slicing.

DARK GREEN KALE WITH CREAMY DILL DRESSING

Before the first frost, kale can be a bit tough. Boiling greens make them tenderer and sweeter since some of their bitterness is discarded with the water. However, some nutrients are discarded as well. If preferred, cook the kale in 1/2 inch water for 30 -45 minutes instead. The creamy, rich, yet mild dressing complements the greens and supports the rest of the menu.

1 pound kale
2 quarts water

Bring 2 quarts water to a boil in a big pot. Submerge the kale in the boiling water for 5 minutes. Drain and cool the kale. Cut out inside stem. Return stems to the pot and boil for an additional 5 minutes.

Cut stems and kale finely. Fluff them together in a bowl. Pour dill dressing over kale just before serving.

CREAMY DILL DRESSING

1 egg
1 tablespoon mustard
1 tablespoon apple cider vinegar
1/2 teaspoon sea salt
1 tablespoon maple syrup
1 cup extra virgin olive oil
1/4 teaspoon rosemary powder
2 tablespoons dried dill weed

In blender or food processor combine egg, mustard, vinegar, salt and maple syrup. While blender is running low, slowly add oil. The dressing will thicken. Add rosemary and dill weed. Let the dressing rest for 1/2 hour for flavors to merge.

RADISH CHRYSANTHEMUMS

These simple, beautiful radish chrysanthemum pickles lighten up the meal. They are a delight for the eye and aid digestion. The radish flowers are marinated in the fermented brine of the Japanese umeboshi plums. Two tablespoons raw apple cider vinegar and 1 teaspoon salt can be used instead

8-10 round radishes or 1 medium daikon radish
2 tablespoons umeboshi vinegar.

Cut the radishes into chrysanthemum shapes.

Place the radishes in a jar. Add cool water and let them sit in the refrigerator for several hours. The radish flowers will spread out in cold water.

Before serving, sprinkle a dash of umeboshi vinegar on each radish flower and, with your hands, help them unfold completely.

DANISH APPLE DELIGHT

The Danish apple dessert is very refreshing and easy to make. It is delicious as it is or served with whipped cream, yogurt or kefir made of fresh raw dairy.

2 quarts of sweet apples cored and cut in half moons
1/2 cup water
1 dash sea salt
3 tablespoons butter
1/2 cup extra virgin olive oil
3 cups fine breadcrumbs from sourdough bread
3/4 cup maple syrup
Whipped cream
Fruit sweetened jam for garnish

Place the apples in a pan with water and salt. Bring to a boil, cover and simmer for 10 minutes.

Meanwhile heat a frying pan. Add the butter and oil. Sautee the bread crumbs until all the oil and butter mixture is absorbed evenly. Add maple syrup and sauté while stirring for 2 minutes.

In a 9 x 9 inches serving dish layer uniformly half the apples, then half the bread crumb mixture, then apples and end with breadcrumb mixture. Press the surface gently with a spoon and let dessert rest for 1 hour.

Garnish the apple dessert decoratively with raw whipped cream and fruit jam before serving.

NOURISHING THE INNER LIGHT— COOKING FOR WINTER

The sky hangs like a veil of ephemeral colors over a blanket of countless beautiful, star-shaped snowflakes. It is quiet in the garden. There is no movement; nothing is stirring. All life seems to have left. Where has it gone? I reflect on my life with what feels like the transparency of ice, and envision my intentions for the coming year. Like the seeds embedded in the sheltering ground, I protect these intentions in a bosom of warmth and hope.

As I leave my garden to go inside, I notice frosty crystal patterns of ice flowers decorating the windowpane. These lovely pictures reveal beautifully the invisible life forces so active at other times of the year.

On our south-facing porch is a small selection of herbs we transplanted in the fall. Their fresh dark green colors, magnificent flavor, and healing properties enhance many of our winter meals.

On our north-facing porch we store sacks of golden grains. I let my fingers run through the sun-ripened wheat. If kept in a dry, cool place they will be able to sprout, in many years to come, without giving themselves up to the forces of decay, like the rest of the plant world.

Although the winter vegetables and grains rest calmly in storage during most of the winter, my kitchen is forever alive and vibrating. On the counter stand a couple of jars with fizzing kombucha and kvass, next to a crock with sauerkraut-to-be. Something is always brewing and bubbling with life. Behind the wood stove are more crocks. In these, homemade miso is aging. Miso making is a very long process that can take up to several years to finish, whereas the sourdough bread near the stove is slowly rising, getting ready to be baked in just a few hours.

 Explore

Kombucha is a stimulating, delicious, and refreshing brew originating from the Russian mountains. Order kombucha starter from mail order, or receive one from a friend. Make about 4 quarts of sweetened tea in a gallon glass jar, using 3 tablespoons black or green tea and 1/2 cup raw sugar. Add 1 teaspoon sea salt and 1/2 cup grated ginger. When the tea has cooled, strain it into another sterilized glass jar. Place the kombucha starter on top, cover the jar with a towel, and let it sit in a very warm place (72-100 degrees). The fizzy, lightly sour and spicy brew is ready after about one to four weeks, or when another pancake-like starter is created. Dilute the kombucha with water to taste before serving.

WINTER MENUS

These winter menus bring strength and vitality. They stimulate inner warmth, calmness, and motivation. They are full of flavor, nutritious and wholesome. The attractiveness of each meal comes from its beauty, simplicity, and vigor.

EARLY WINTER MENU

Venison and Vegetable Soup with Sage
Millet and Quinoa with Mushroom Sauce
Winter Squash and Sweet Potato Medley
Brussels Sprouts in Sweet and Sour Dressing
Pressed Apple Celery Salad with Walnuts

CELEBRATION OF WINTER MENU

Hot Spiced Glogg
French Onion Soup with Fried Sourdough Bread
Refried Rice with Parsley
Sautéed Chicken Breast in Golden Ginger Sauce
Baked Herbed Beans
Walnut Breaded Celeriac Root
Roasted Squash with Rosemary
Green Kale with Herbed Yogurt Dressing
Cranberry Apple Relish
Spiced Star Cookies

LATE WINTER MENU

Yellow Split Pea Soup with Caraway Seeds
Rye Bread and Fresh Butter
Baked Rice and Squash with Roasted Pecans
Green Kale Pickles with Ginger

EARLY WINTER MENU

Venison and Vegetable Soup with Sage
Millet and Quinoa with Mushroom Sauce
Winter Squash and Sweet Potato Medley
Brussels Sprouts in Sweet and Sour Dressing
Pressed Apple Celery Salad with Walnuts

The grains and walnuts need soaking for 4–8 hours. Wash and cut the vegetables. Press the salad. While the grains and the squash cook, make the soup, cook the brussels sprouts, and blend the dressing. Serve the soup with the meal.

VENISON AND VEGETABLE SOUP WITH SAGE

The cold weather in the north calls for warming soups. Venison can be substituted with any meat or fried tempeh. This soup is light compared to bean soups and stews. It complements the more substantial grains and vegetables in the rest of the meal.

2-4 tablespoons extra virgin olive oil or butter
1 pound of venison (beef or lamb), thinly sliced
1 leek, cut in fine diagonals
2 cloves garlic, minced
1 carrot, diced
1 celery stalk, diced
1/2 tablespoon dried sage
1/2 tablespoon dried thyme
1 bay leaf
1 quart soup stock
1/2 to 1 tablespoon sea salt
Dashes of pepper
2 tablespoons parsley, chopped fine, for garnish

Heat a large soup pot, and then add oil to sauté meat until lightly browned. Add leeks and garlic and sauté for 1 minute. Then add carrots and celery and sauté for 1 minute.

Place the sage, thyme and bay leaf in cheesecloth or a cotton tea bag. Add bag to vegetables with the soup stock. Cover the pot and bring it to a boil. Lower the heat and simmer for 6-10 minutes.

Remove the herbal sachet. Season the soup with salt and pepper. Simmer for a few minutes.

Serve hot, garnished with parsley.

MILLET AND QUINOA WITH MUSHROOM SAUCE

Both millet and quinoa cook in a short time. When soaked first they become sweeter, softer and lighter. I use mushrooms in cooking mainly for their medicinal properties. The shitake mushrooms can be substituted with other types of mushrooms.

1 cup millet

1 cup quinoa

4 1/2 to 5 cups water

1 teaspoon vinegar or juice from cultured vegetables

2 pinches of sea salt

Soak the millet and quinoa for 4-8 hours in water and vinegar. Bring it to a boil. Add salt. Keep the cover ajar and let it simmer for 20 minutes. Turn off heat and let the grains rest for 10 minutes in the pot before serving hot with mushroom sauce.

(Mushroom Sauce recipe continues on next page)

MUSHROOM SAUCE

2 1/2 cups water or soup stock (see Soups)
2 cups dried shitake mushrooms
4 tablespoons extra virgin olive oil or butter
1 big onion, minced
1/4 cup whole wheat pastry flour or unbleached white wheat flour
1 teaspoon lemon juice
Salt and pepper

Bring the water or stock to a boil and turn off the heat. Add shitake and let them soak for 20 minutes. Spoon out the mushrooms, trim the ends off and discard. Slice shitake mushrooms into thin strips and return to stock. Let it simmer for 10 minutes.

In a heavy-bottomed saucepan, gently heat oil or butter. Add onions and sauté over medium heat until translucent. Add flour and sauté for 2 minutes. Stir the hot mushroom stock into the flour onion mixture. Whisk it gently. Add shitake mushrooms. Cover the pan, and let it simmer over for 5-10 minutes. Stir occasionally.

Season the sauce with lemon juice, salt and pepper. Serve hot over the grains.

WINTER SQUASH AND SWEET POTATO MEDLEY

These sweet vegetables are cooked for a long time with little water and a dash of salt. The salt, kombu and cooking method create a sweet, flavorful and strong dish. Many enjoy the peel of squash and sweet potato, so leave it on if it is tender, or use the peel for soup stocks.

2 cups winter squash, cut in chunks

1 cup sweet potato, cut in chunks

3 inches kombu (optional), cut into strips about 1/4 inch wide

1 cup water

1/2 teaspoon sea salt

1 tablespoon tamari soy sauce

Place the squash and sweet potato in a pot on top of the kombu. Add water and salt and bring to a boil. Cover the pot, turn down the heat and simmer for 20 minutes.

Add tamari soy sauce, place the lid back on and gently shake the pot a couple of times. Simmer for 2 minutes.

If any liquid is left in the pot, take off the lid. Cook until all flavors and liquids are absorbed. Discard the kombu or serve, seasoned with dashes of tamari soy sauce, with the squash and sweet potatoes.

BRUSSELS SPROUTS IN SWEET AND SOUR DRESSING

Brussels sprouts are delicious in this recipe with nutmeg and vinegar. Cook them until they are tender, yet still crunchy, and have a bright green color.

2 cups brussels sprouts
1/2 teaspoon sea salt

Trim ends off the brussels sprouts and remove outer leaves. If the brussels sprouts are large cut them in halves or quarter them.

Bring 1 quart of water to a boil. Add salt and brussels sprouts and cook uncovered for about 5 minutes.

Drain the brussels sprouts. Mix them with the dressing and let them marinate for 30 minutes.

SWEET AND SOUR DRESSING

1 tablespoon vinegar
1/2 teaspoon nutmeg, freshly grated
1 tablespoon raw honey
1 tablespoon mustard
1 tablespoon water

In a medium-sized bowl whisk together vinegar, nutmeg, mustard and honey. Then add the water. Mix well before serving.

PRESSED APPLE CELERY SALAD WITH WALNUTS

A pressed salad is refreshing in the winter, to lighten up the meal. The walnuts taste freshly shelled when they have been soaked. The pressure and salt "cooks" the food without heat, and makes the vegetables more digestible and delicious. The apples can be substituted with Chinese cabbage.

1/2 cup walnuts
1/2 tablespoon sea salt
2 large sweet firm apples, cored and cut in thin slices
2 stalks celery, cut in thin diagonals
4 slices of orange

Soak the nuts for 4-8 hours in lightly salted water.

Mix salt with apples and celery. Place the mixture under pressure. Use a pickle press or two bowls, a smaller bowl inside a larger one. Place the vegetables between the bowls. Lay a heavy weight in the smaller bowl. Let it sit for 20 minutes to 2 hours.

Drain off the liquid that has been drawn out of the vegetables by the salt.

Drain, rinse, and cut the nuts fine. Add them to vegetables and mix well. Serve a few tablespoons per person on a slice of orange.

CELEBRATION OF WINTER MENU

Hot Spiced Glogg

French Onion Soup with Fried Sourdough Bread

Refried Rice with Parsley

Sautéed Chicken Breast in Golden Ginger Sauce

Baked Herbed Beans

Walnut Breaded Celeriac Root

Roasted Squash with Rosemary

Green Kale with Herbed Yogurt Dressing

Cranberry Apple Relish

Spiced Star Cookies

Soak the beans overnight. Prepare the dough for cookies while cooking the beans. Soak walnuts and rice. Bake the cookies and the beans. While the grains are simmering, and the squash baking, start the soup and prepare the rest of the vegetables. Cook the kale and mix the dressing. Make the relish and store it cold. Fry the celeriac, sauté the chicken, and prepare the sauce. Leave most of the dishes in a warm oven until ready to serve.

HOT SPICED GLOGG

Hot, spiced winter drinks are common in many countries. They are often made with red wine and strong liquor. Red berry juices made with blueberries or elderberries are a healthier alternative. Serve in small glasses.

1/2 cup almonds
2 cups water
1 quart red wine or 1 quart dark berry juice
   (see Blossoming and Maturing—Cooking for Summer)
1 tablespoon cloves
3–4 whole cinnamon sticks
1/2 cup raisins
1 orange cut in slices

Boil 2 cups water and pour over the almonds. Let it sit for 10 minutes. Slip peels off the almonds and cut in thin diagonals.

Meanwhile slowly heat the juice or wine in a big pot with cinnamon sticks, cloves and raisins. Add almonds, cover with a lid and let it simmer for 20 minutes.

Serve in small glasses or mugs with a spoon. Garnish with orange slices.

**FRENCH ONION SOUP WITH FRIED
SOURDOUGH BREAD**

This rich soup gets its round and full flavors from the browning of the onions.

1/2 cup water
2 pounds yellow onions, cut in crescent moons
8 tablespoons extra virgin olive oil or butter
2 cloves of garlic minced, and 1 whole clove garlic
1 quart nourishing soup stock (see Soups)
4 bay leaves
1 tablespoon dried thyme
2 slices of sourdough bread cut in quarters
2 tablespoons tamari soy sauce
1/2 teaspoon sea salt
2 tablespoons maple syrup
2 dashes of pepper
Parmesan and minced parsley for garnish

Bring half a cup of water to a boil in a saucepan. Add onions. Steam over medium heat for 4 minutes, or until onions are softening. Place the onions in a bowl.

While the saucepan is hot, heat 2 tablespoons oil or butter. Add onions and sauté for 15 minutes over medium heat until brown. Stir from time to time. Add minced garlic, stock, bay leaves and thyme. Bring the soup to a boil and let it simmer, covered for 15 minutes. Remove bay leaves.

Cut the whole garlic in half. Rub both sides of bread quarters with garlic.

In a frying pan heat another 3 tablespoons of oil or butter. Fry the bread on one side, over medium heat, until golden. Add the last 3 tablespoons oil and fry the other side. Set the bread aside.

Season the soup with tamari soy sauce, salt, maple syrup and pepper. Simmer one minute.

Pour the soup in individual serving bowls. Place the bread on top of the soup, garnish with Parmesan and parsley. Serve immediately.

REFRIED RICE WITH PARSLEY

Refrying is a second cooking method applied to grains or beans that have already been cooked. Vegetables, herbs and spices can be fried in the oil first, before adding the rice. Seasoning is done at the end of the cooking time. The longer the grains are fried, and the more oil that is used, the crustier the grain becomes. In this dish, the rice is fried a short time in little oil to make it crisp, but soft. Make decorative small rice balls and fry them the same way. The dark rich sesame oil adds substance and subtle flavor to the rice.

3 tablespoons dark roasted sesame oil or extra virgin olive oil

3 cups cooked brown rice

1/4 cup chopped parsley

2 tablespoons tamari soy sauce

Heat a skillet over medium heat. Coat the bottom of the skillet with oil.

Add the rice and fry covered for 5 minutes, turning occasionally with a spatula.

Sprinkle parsley over the rice, season with tamari soy sauce and simmer uncovered for 2 minutes.

SAUTÉED CHICKEN BREAST IN GOLDEN GINGER SAUCE

The chicken breasts are tender and lightly seasoned with ginger, so that the herbs are not overpowered. Instead of chicken breasts use a whole, parted chicken, or sliced firm tofu fried in 1/4 cup extra virgin olive oil until golden.

4-8 chicken breasts, cut in half

1 teaspoon turmeric

1/4 teaspoon dried thyme, crumbled

1/4 teaspoon dried tarragon, crumbled (optional)

1/2 teaspoon sea salt

Dash of pepper

3 tablespoons extra virgin olive oil or butter

1/4 cup shallots or yellow onions, finely chopped

1/2 cup soup stock (see Soups) or water

1 teaspoon cornstarch or arrowroot diluted in 2 tablespoon water

Sea salt to taste

1/2 to 1 tablespoon ginger juice, squeezed from grated ginger

Place chicken breasts between two sheets of waxed paper. Pound until they are 1/4 inch thick. Sprinkle with turmeric, thyme, tarragon, salt and pepper.

Heat a skillet and add the oil or butter. Sauté the shallots for 2 minutes, then add the chicken breast and sauté for 2-3 minutes on each side, until browned. Add the light soup stock. Cook chicken for 2 minutes more.

Pour diluted arrowroot or cornstarch into the skillet. Cook 1 minute more or until the sauce becomes translucent.

Season the sauce with salt. Remove from heat and stir in the ginger juice. Serve hot.

BAKED HERBED BEANS

This is one of the dishes that taste better after the flavors blend overnight. Make a double batch and serve the following day with bread and sauerkraut.

1 cup dried pinto beans, cleaned, rinsed, and soaked for 12 hours

3-4 cups water

3 inches kombu sea vegetable

2 onions, minced

1 tablespoon light miso

1 tablespoon vinegar

4 tablespoons apple butter

1/2 tablespoon dried or 1 tablespoon fresh, minced rosemary

1/2 tablespoon dried or 1 tablespoon fresh, minced sage

Drain the beans and discard the soaking water. Place the beans in a pot with 3 cups fresh water and bring to a boil. Skim off the foam that arises. Add kombu, cover the pot and simmer for 2-4 hours, or until beans are completely tender. Add water from time to time if necessary.

Preheat the oven to 350 degrees.

Drain the beans. Reserve 1 cup of cooking liquid.

In a 2 quart casserole, combine 1 cup cooking liquid with onions, miso, vinegar, and apple butter. Add beans and herbs. Mix well. Cover the casserole and bake for 1 hour.

WALNUT BREADED CELERIAC ROOT

The celeriac root has a unique flavor. I use celeriac in soup stocks, roast or fry it, with or without the crispy breading.

1/2 cup walnuts

1 egg

1 to 1 1/2 cups roasted breadcrumbs

1/2 teaspoon sea salt

1 dash of pepper

1 big celery root, peeled and sliced in thick rounds, then quartered

1/2 cup whole wheat pastry flour

1/4 cup extra virgin olive oil or butter

Soak the walnuts for 6-8 hours in lightly salted water. Drain and finely chop the nuts.

Beat the egg in a flat dish.

On parchment paper mix the breadcrumbs, walnuts, salt and pepper.

Place flour on another piece of parchment paper. Coat each piece of celeriac first in flour, then egg mixture, and last with the breadcrumb mixture.

Heat a frying pan, and add oil or butter. Fry the celery piece about 5-7 minutes on each side until the breading is golden and the celeriac tender. Serve hot.

ROASTED SQUASH WITH ROSEMARY

The rosemary flavored squash slices are deliciously sweet, slightly salty and crispy. Potatoes are also delicious cooked this way.

1 small butternut squash
6 tablespoons extra virgin olive oil or smelted butter
4 tablespoons dried rosemary
Dashes of sea salt and pepper

Preheat the oven to 400 degrees.

Peel and cut the squash in less than 1/4 inch thick slices. In a roasting pan layer the slices in rows overlapping each other.

Drizzle oil or butter over the squash and sprinkle evenly with rosemary, salt and pepper.

Roast in the oven for 20-30 minutes or until soft and crispy. Serve hot.

GREEN KALE WITH HERBED YOGURT DRESSING

Lacinato kale is deep green and very hardy. The stems can be left on the kale. The tangy dressing complements the kale and brings out its richness.

1/2 cup water

1 dash sea salt

1/2 pound lacinato kale leaves

Bring the water to a boil. Add salt.

Cut the stems from the greens, and discard. Cut the greens in fine diagonals.

Add the leaves to the boiling water and cook for 15-30 minutes.

Drain the greens for any remaining liquid. Pour the dressing over the greens right before serving.

HERBED YOGURT DRESSING

1 cup yogurt (see Late Spring Menu)

2 teaspoons mustard

1 egg (optional)

2 tablespoons dried herbs such as dill, rosemary, marjoram and thyme

1/2 teaspoon sea salt

Blend or whisk all the ingredients well together. Let the dressing rest for 1 hour before serving.

CRANBERRY APPLE RELISH

This relish is beautiful and refreshing. Its red color, sweet and bitter flavors, and crunchy raw texture complement the meal well. Add at times cinnamon and cloves, or use a lemon instead of the orange.

1 orange
12 ounces cranberries, rinsed and cleaned well
2 apples cored and sliced
1 tablespoon maple syrup
1/4 teaspoon sea salt

Grate the orange rind and set it aside.

Place the cranberries in a food processor. Chop the cranberries coarsely. While the food processor is running, add apples, 2-3 tablespoons orange juice, orange peel, maple syrup and salt. Blend for a few minutes. Store relish cold until ready to serve.

SPICED STAR COOKIES

These cookies are fun to make. Instead of serving them on a plate, I pinch a hole through one of the rays of the star, string a red ribbon through it, and hang the cookies decoratively on the Christmas tree or on a dowel.

3 cups whole wheat pastry flour
1/2 teaspoon baking soda
1/2 teaspoon sea salt
1/2 tablespoon ground cinnamon
1 tablespoon ground dried ginger or 2 tablespoon fresh ginger juice
1/2 teaspoon ground cloves
1/2 teaspoon ground nutmeg
1/3 cup cold pressed olive oil
1/2 cup maple syrup
1 tablespoon vinegar
1/2 cup molasses
1 egg

Sift the flour, baking soda, salt and spices into a mixing bowl.

Combine oil, maple syrup, vinegar, molasses and egg. Add to the flour mixture and blend well to make a soft dough. Wrap the dough in a plastic bag or foil, and leave it in refrigerator overnight.

Preheat the oven to 350 degrees.

On a lightly floured surface, roll out half the dough, to about eighth inch thickness. Cut with cookie cutters, or with a knife, into stars. Make a hole if hanging the star.

Place the cookies on un-greased cookie sheet, leaving space around each cookie. Bake them for 5-6 minutes, or until cookies are firm but not browning. Move to wire rack with a spatula. Let the cookies cool completely.

Place ribbons in each star and hang them decoratively.

LATE WINTER MENU

Yellow Split Pea Soup with Caraway Seeds
Rye Bread with Fresh Butter
Baked Rice and Squash with Roasted Pecans
Green Kale Pickles with Ginger

The green kale pickles need to be made a few days in advance. The rye bread is best if it rests for a day. The split peas need to soak for 8 hours. While baking the rice, churn the butter, finish the soup, and serve.

YELLOW SPLIT PEA SOUP WITH CARAWAY SEEDS

Split pea soup is a very common dish in Scandinavia, eaten weekly during the winter months. It is typically served with smoked sausages and the delicious staple of northern Europe, dark rye bread.

1 1/2 cups yellow split peas
1 1/2 quarts soup stock (see Soups)
2 tablespoons extra virgin olive oil or butter
1 tablespoon whole caraway seeds
2 tablespoons dried thyme
1/2 to 1 tablespoon sea salt
1 big onion diced
1 big carrot cut into flowers
1 tablespoon chives or scallions cut thin

Soak the split peas in water for 8-12 hours.

Drain split peas, place in a pot and add the soup stock. Bring to a boil. Skim off foam on the surface. Cover and simmer for 1 hour or until split peas are completely soft.

Heat a small saucepan; add oil or butter and sauté caraway seeds and onions for 3 minutes.

Add thyme, salt, onion and carrots to the split peas. Add more water if necessary. Cover and simmer for 30 minutes. Stir occasionally.

Serve in individual bowls and garnish with scallions or chives.

RYE BREAD WITH FRESH BUTTER

The rye bread is delicious served with butter or as open-faced sandwiches. Pickled herring or raw cheeses complement the bread wonderfully. Use whole wheat sourdough starter or make a separate mother dough of rye flour.

3 cups sourdough starter (mother dough)
2 cups water
1 tablespoon sea salt
1/4 cup barley malt or sorghum
4 cups rye flour

Follow instructions for sourdough bread (see Celebrating Summer). Use two cups sourdough starter for the rye bread and set aside one cup starter for next baking. The dough for the rye bread will be moister than whole wheat sourdough bread. It is not kneaded. It is spooned into baking pans and evened out with a wet spatula. The bread pan should only be half filled, since the dough will double its size after second rising.

FRESH BUTTER

2 cups fresh raw cream or whipping cream
1/4 to 1/2 teaspoon sea salt

Pour cream into a two-quart glass jar and cover tightly. Rhythmically shake the jar up and down until the butter separates from the buttermilk into one big lump. This can take 1/2 to 3/4 hour. Pour off the buttermilk and use for cakes or waffles.

Place butter in a bowl. Stir in salt and drain any excess liquid that should appear.

BAKED RICE AND SQUASH WITH ROASTED PECANS

Sometimes I dry-roast the rice before baking it. It makes the dish stronger, and adds a nutty flavor that complements the sweet squash. Add boiling water, without soaking the rice first, for a chewier dish. At times substitute the water with red roibos tea or soup stock. Use soaked and dry-roasted walnuts or other nuts instead of pecans.

2 cups brown rice, soaked in 4 cups water

3 tablespoons pecans, soaked in one cup water

2 teaspoons vinegar or juice from cultured vegetables

2 cups winter squash, peeled and diced large

1/4 teaspoon sea salt

Rinse and soak the rice and pecans separately in water with one teaspoon vinegar for 4-8 hours.

Preheat the oven to 350 degrees.

Place the rice and soaking water in a baking dish with the squash and salt. Cover the dish and bake for 60 minutes. Remove the rice from the oven and let it sit for 10 minutes while roasting the pecans.

Chop the pecans and sprinkle them over the rice before serving.

GREEN KALE PICKLES WITH GINGER

The kale pickles are refreshing and warming. Use different greens and add a grated carrot or carrot flower for color.

1 pound green kale
5 tablespoons sesame seeds
1 tablespoon grated ginger
2 1/2 cups water
3/4 cup tamari soy sauce
3 tablespoons rice malt

Clean and rinse the kale. Cut out the stem, discard or use it thinly sliced in a stir-fry. Cut the kale in thin diagonals and place in a wide mouth quart jar.

Soak sesame seeds for 5 minutes and drain.

Heat a skillet and dry-roast the sesame seeds while stirring rhythmically, until the seeds can be easily crushed between thumb and ring finger. Pour the seeds into a bowl to cool before adding them to the kale.

Grate the ginger and place the juicy pulp on top of the kale and seeds.

Combine water, tamari soy sauce and rice syrup in a saucepan. Heat to just below boiling. Pour liquid over the kale. Add more water if necessary to cover the greens. Cover the jar and let it sit, cold, for 2-5 days.

Serve a couple of tablespoons of the pickled kale for each person with the meal.

RECIPE INDEX

SOUPS

Barley Mushroom Soup with Scallions	96
Consommé with Snap Peas and Chives	76
Cool Refreshing Lemon Dill Cucumber Soup	126
Cumin Lentil Stew with Lemon Balm	154
French Onion Soup with Fried Sourdough Bread	172
Light Vegetable Soup with Dill	83
Tamari Soup with Cauliflower and Lemon	105
Venison and Vegetable Soup with Sage	164
Yellow Split Pea Soup with Caraway Seeds	182
Zesty Fish Soup with Scallions	135

GRAIN DISHES AND BREADS

Baked Rice and Squash with Roasted Pecans	184
Crunchy Rice and Wheat Berries with Sesame Salt	84
Cucumber Rice Rolls with Dipping Sauce	118
Golden Polenta Triangles	127
Golden Rice Pilaf	136
Millet and Quinoa with Mushroom Sauce	165
Millet Squash Pie with Parsley and Roasted Walnuts	155
Pasta Rolls with Creamy Parsley	119
Refried Rice with Parsley	173
Rice with Black Olives	77
Rice with Grated Carrots, Parsley, and Sunflower Seeds	106
Rye Bread	183
Whole Wheat Sourdough Bread	115, 116
Zucchini Corn Muffins with Olive Basil Dip	146

DISHES WITH BEANS, FISH, OR ANIMAL FOODS

Baked Herbed Beans — 175
Broiled Salmon with Thyme — 78
Cumin Lentil Stew with Lemon Balm — 154
Fried Crispy Tempeh — 147
Herbed Hummus — 117
Herbed Tofu Rolls with Ginger Sauce — 86
Paprika Eggs with Scallions and Miso Mayonnaise — 87
Poached Cod with Lemon Paprika — 107
Roasted Maple Turkey — 145
Sautéed Chicken Breast in Golden Ginger Sauce — 174
Sautéed Scallops in Garlic — 88
Spicy Kidney Beans — 128
Summer Shish Kebab — 121
Venison and Vegetable Soup with Sage — 164
Yellow Split Pea Soup with Caraway Seeds — 182
Zesty Fish Soup with Scallions — 135

VEGETABLE SIDE DISHES

Arame Sea Vegetables with Orange Rind — 92
Baked Hiziki Rolls with Orange Rind — 156
Boiled Crunchy Salad with Goddess Dressing — 138
Brussels Sprouts in Sweet and Sour Dressing — 168
Butter Drizzled Steamed Asparagus — 89
Collard Greens with Orange Dressing — 149
Colorful Brine Pickles Salad with Vinaigrette — 129
Dark Green Kale with Creamy Dill Dressing — 157
Fried Yellow Squash Rounds — 109
Green Arugula Salad with Sweet Vinegar Miso Dressing — 97
Green Beans with Butter and Garlic — 148
Green Kale with Herbed Yogurt Dressing — 178
Green Rounds with Peanut Sauce — 122
Grilled Caraway Beets and Red Onions — 139
Grilled Sweet Corn in the Husk — 120
Holiday Root Medley with Rosemary — 150
Lemon Carrot Salad — 81
New Potatoes with Dill Butter — 108
Pressed New Radishes — 94

Roasted Squash with Rosemary   177
Rosemary Stuffed Mushrooms   90
Sautéed Radishes and Greens with Sesame Seeds   80
Spring Burdock and Nettles with Cilantro   91
Steamed Broccoli with Honey Mustard Dressing   79
Steamed Tender Leeks with Parsley Butter   137
Stuffed Herbed Buttercup Squash   144
Summer Shish Kebab   121
Walnut Breaded Celeriac Root   176
Wild Green Sautee   93
Winter Squash and Sweet Potato Medley   167
Young Summer Greens with Mustard Dressing   110

SAUCES, CONDIMENTS, SPREADS, AND DRESSINGS

Creamy Dill Dressing   157
Dipping Sauce   119
Fall Herbed Vinegar   131
Flaxseed Condiment   65
Fresh Butter   183
Goddess Dressing   138
Golden Ginger Sauce   174
Herbed Hummus   117
Herbed Yogurt Dressing   178
Honey Mustard Dressing   79
Mayonnaise   88
Miso Mayonnaise   87
Mushroom Sauce   166
Mustard Dressing   110
Olive Basil Dip   146
Orange Dressing   149
Peanut Sauce   122
Sesame Salt   85
Sesame Seeds   80
Spiced Cranberry Chutney   151
Sweet and Sour Dressing   168
Sweet Vinegar Miso Dressing   97
Vinaigrette   129

CULTURED, FERMENTED FOODS AND CONDIMENTS

Carrot Flower Pickles   111
Cranberry Apple Relish   179
Colorful Brine Pickles   129
Ginger Kombucha   161
Green Kale Pickles with Ginger   185
Juicy Sauerkraut   140
Kefir   123
Kvass Autumn Refresher   143
Pressed Apple Celery Salad with Walnuts   169
Pressed Radishes   94
Radish Chrysanthemums   158
Tamari Pickled Onions   152
Yogurt   99

DESSERTS AND BEVERAGES

Almond Yogurt Dessert   99
Baked Cinnamon Apples   141
Danish Apple Delight   159
Dark Berry Juice   101
Ginger Kombucha   161
Hot Spiced Glogg   171
Kefir Lemon Cooler   123
Kvass Autumn Refresher   143
Nettle Infusion   73
Oatmeal Cookies   98
Spiced Star Cookies   180
Sweet Sticky Blueberry Nut Bars   124
Summer Spritzer   114
Sun Tea with Lemon Balm   112

BIBLIOGRAPHY

Adams and Whitcher, *The Plant Between the Sun and the Earth*. Boulder: Shambhala, 1982.

Anderson, Adrian, *Living a Spiritual Year*. Gordon: Threshold Publishing, 1993.

Bitttleston, Adam, *Our Spiritual Companions*. Edinburgh: Floris Books, 1980.

Bockenmuhl, Jochen, *In Partnership with Nature*. Wyoming: Biodynamic Literature, 1981.

Chopra, Deepak, *The Love Poems of Rumi*. New York: Harmony Books, 1998.

Cook, Wendy E., *Foodwise*. East Sussex: Clairview, 2003.

Colquhoun and Ewald, *New Eyes for Plant*. Stroud: Hawthorne House, 1996.

Fuyoko, Masanobu, *One Straw Revolution*. Emmaus: Rodale Press, 1978.

Goethe, Johann Wolfgang von, *The Metamorphosis of Plant*. Kimberton: Biodynamic Farming and Gardening Associations, Inc., 1993.

Hauschka, Rudolf, *The Nature of Substance*. East Sussex: Sophia Books, 2002.

Hauschka, Rudolf, *Nutrition*. East Sussex: Sophia Books, 2002.

Hiebel, Frederick, *Message of Beauty*. Fair Oaks: St. George Publications, 1991.

Jack, Alex, *Let Food Be Thy Medicine*. Becket: One Peaceful World Press, 1999.

Jack, Alex, *Chewing Made Easy*. Becket: Macrobiotic Path, 2006.

Kervran, C. Louis, *Biological Transformations*. Magalia: Happiness Press, 1998.

Klocek, Dennis, *Seeking Spirit Vision*. Fair Oaks: Rudolf Steiner College Press, 2001.

Klocek, Dennis, *A Biodynamic Book of Moons*. Wyoming: Biodynamic Literature, 1983.

Koepf, Herbert, *The Biodynamic Farm*. Hudson: Anthroposophical Press, 1989.

Kolin and Mafi, *Rumi Hidden Music*. London: Element, 2001.

Kolisko, Eugen, *Nutrition No. 1 and No. 2*. Bournemouth: Kolisko Archive Publications, 1978.

Kingsolver, Barbara, *Animal, Vegetable Miracle*. New York: HarperCollins, 2007.

Kushi, Michio, *The Macrobiotic Path to Total Health*. New York: Ballantine Books, 2003.

Langre, Jacques de, *The Hidden Power of Sea Salt*. Magalia: The Grain and Salt Society Publisher, 1985.

Levy, Juliette de Bairacli, *Common Herbs for Natural Health*. Woodstock: Ash Tree Publishing, 1997.

Maybey, Richard, *The New Age Herbalist*. New York: Simon and Schuster, 1988.

Moore, Thomas, *Care of the Soul*. New York: HarperPerennial, 1994.

Moore, Thomas, *Re-Enchantment of Everyday Life*. New York: HarperCollins Publishers, 1996.

Naydler, Jeremy, *Goethe on Science*. Edinburgh: Floris Books, 1996.

Pfeiffer, EhenFried E., *Does Bread Nourish*. Magalia: Happiness Press, 1978.

Pollan, Michael, *Omnivore's Dilemma*. New York: Penguin Books, 2007.

Pollan, Michael, *Botany of Desire*. New York: Random House, 2001.

Price, Weston, *Nutrition and Physical Degeneration*. La Mesa: The Price-Pottenger Nutrition Foundation, Inc., 1970.

Proctor, Peter, *Grasp the Nettle*. New Zealand: Random House New Zealand Ltd, 1997.

Renzenbrink, Udo, *Diet and Cancer*. London: Rudolf Steiner Press, 1988.

Romunde, R. van, *Perceiving Plants*. United States: Jannebeth Roell, 1999.

Sardello, Robert, *Facing the World with Soul*. Hudson: Lindisfarne Press, 1992.

Sardello, Robert, *Freeing the World from Fear*. New York: Riverhead Books, 1999.

Sardello, Robert, *Love and the World*. Hudson: Lindisfarne Press, 2001.

Sardello, Robert, *The Power of Soul*. Charlottesville: Hampton Roads Publishing, 1999.

Sardello, Robert, *Silence*. Benson: Goldenstone Press, 2006.

Schilthuis, Willy, *Biodynamic Agriculture*. Hudson: Anthroposophical Press, 1994.

Schmidt, Gerhard, *Cancer and Nutrition*. Spring Valley: Anthroposophical Press, 1986.

Schmidt, Gerhard, *The Dynamic of Nutrition*. Wyoming: Biodynamic Literature, 1980.

Schmidt, Gerhard, *The Essentials of Nutrition*. Wyoming: Biodynamic Literature, 1987.

Schwenk, Theodor, *Sensitive Chaos*. London: Rudolf Steiner Press, 1996.

Soesman, Albert, *Our Twelve Senses*. Stroud: Hawthorne Press, 1988.

Steiner, Rudolf, *Agriculture*. Kimberton: Biodynamic Farming and Gardening Associations, Inc., 1993.

Steiner, Rudolf, *The Boundaries of Natural Science.* Spring
Valley: Anthroposophical Press, 1983.

Steiner, Rudolf, *The Cycle of the Year.* Hudson: Anthroposophical Press, 1984.

Steiner, Rudolf, *The Goddess.* East Sussex: Sophia Books, 2001.

Steiner, Rudolf, *Guidance in Esoteric Training.* London: Rudolf Steiner Press, 1993

Steiner, Rudolf, *Healing Processes.* Spring Valley: Anthroposophical Press, 2000.

Steiner, Rudolf, *Health and Illness, Volume 1 and 2.* Spring
Valley: Anthroposophical Press, 1981.

Steiner, Rudolf, *Learning to See into the Spiritual World.*
Hudson: Anthroposophical Press, 1990.

Steiner, Rudolf, *The Light Course.* Worcester England:
Goethean Science Foundation, 1948.

Steiner, Rudolf, *Man and the Nature Spirits.* Spring Valley: Mercury Press, 1983.

Steiner, Rudolf, *Man and the World of Stars.* Hudson: Anthroposophical Press, 1963.

Steiner, Rudolf, *Nature Spirits.* London: Rudolf Steiner Press, 1995.

Steiner, Rudolf, *Nutrition and Health.* Hudson: Anthroposophical Press, 1987.

Steiner, Rudolf, *Toward Imagination.* Hudson: Anthroposophical Press, 1990.

Steiner, Rudolf, *The Spirit in the Realm of Plants.* Spring Valley: Mercury Press, 1984.

Steiner, Rudolf, *The Warmth Course.* Spring Valley: Mercury Press, 1980.

Ushio, Moriyasu, *The Ume Plum's Secret.* Magalia: Happiness Press, 1992.

Weed, Susun, *Healing Wise.* Woodstock: Ash Tree Publishing, 1989.

Werner and Stockli, *Life from Light.* Forest Row: Clairview, 2007.

Whitcher, Olive, *The Heart of the Matter.* London: Temple Lodge, 1997.

Whitcher, Olive, *Projective Geometry.* London: Rudolf Steiner Press, 1971.

Whitcher, Olive, *Sunspace.* London: Rudolf Steiner Press, 1989.

Wilkes, John, *Flowforms: The Rhythmical Power of Water.* Edinburgh: Floris Books, 2003.

RECOMMENDED COOKBOOKS

Baum, Lenore, *Lenore's Natural Cuisine.* Farmington Hills: Culinary Press, 1999.

Baum, Lenore, *Sublime Soups.* Farmington Hills: Culinary Press, 2002.

Belleme, Jan and John, *Cooking with Japanese Foods.* Garden
City Park: Avery Publishing Group, 1993.

Colbin, Annemarie, *The Natural Gourmet.* New York: Ballantine Books, 1989.

Cole, Candia Lea, *Gourmet Grains.* Santa Barbara: Woodbridge Press, 1993.

Craze and Jay, *The Tao of Food.* New York: Sterling Publications Company, Inc., 1999.

Erhart and Cerier, *Sea Vegetable Celebration.* Summertown:
Book Publishing Company, 2001.

Esko, Wendy and Ed, *Macrobiotic Cooking for Everyone.*
Tokyo: Japan Publications, Inc., 1983.

Fallon, Sally, *Nourishing Traditions.* San Diego: ProMotion Publishing, 1995.

Frazier, Louise, *Louise's Leaves.* Kimberton: Biodynamic
Farming and Gardening Associations, Inc., 1994.

Hooker, Monique Jamet, *Cooking with the Seasons.* New
York: Henry Holt and Company, Inc., 1997.

Jack, Alex and Gale, *Amber Waves of Grains.* Becket: One Peaceful World Press, 2000.

Kaufmann and Schoneck, *Making Sauerkraut and Pickled Vegetables at Home.*
Summertown: Alive Books, 1997.

Kushi, Aveline, *Aveline Kushi's Complete Guide to Health and Happiness.*
Warner Books, 1985.

Kushi and Esko, *The Changing Seasons Macrobiotic Cookbook.*
Wayne: Avery Publishing Group Inc., 1985.

McCarty, Meredith, *Fresh from a Vegetarian Kitchen.*
Eureka: Turning Point Publications, 1989.

McConnaughey, Evelyn, *Sea Vegetables.* Happy Camp: Naturegraph Publishers, Inc., 1985.

Ohsawa, Lima, *Lima Ohsawa's Macrobiotic Cookbook.* Brookline: Autumn Press, 1974.

Prentice, Jessica, *Full Moon Fest.* White River Junction: Chelsea Green Publishing, 2006.

Renzenbrink and Ljungquist, *Cookery Book from the Lucas Clinic*. Rudolf Steiner Press, 1988.

Saltzman, Joanne, *Amazing Grains*. Tiburon: H J Kramer Inc., 1990.

Shurtleff and Aoyaki, *The Book of Miso*. New York: Ballantine Books, 1982.

Turner, Kristina, *The Self-Healing Cookbook*. Grass Valley: Earthtones Press, 1988.

Waters, Alice, *The Art of Simple Food*. Crown Publishing Group, 2007.

Waters, Alice, *Chez Panisse Menu Cookbook*. Random House Publishing Group, 1995.

Weil and Daley, *The Healthy Kitchen*. London: Ebury Press, 2002.

RESOURCES

SELECTED MAIL ORDER SUPPLIERS

African Red Tea Imports
Beverly Hills, CA 90211
(323) 658-RTEA
www.africanredtea.com

American Miso Company
Ashville, NC 28806-1406
(828) 665-7790
www.great-eastern-sun.com

Eden Foods
701 Tecumseh Road
Clinton, MI, 49236
(888) 424-EDEN
www.edenfoods.com

Gem Culture
Cultures for Miso, Tamari, Kefir,
Yogurt and Kombucha
30301 Sherwood Rd
Fort Bragg, CA 95437
(707) 964-2922
www.gemcultures.com

Gold Mine Natural Food Company
7805 Arjons Dr.
San Diego, CA 92126
(800) 475-3663
www.goldminenaturalfood.com

Green Pastures Dairy and Meats
2353 Broomfield Road
Carlton, MN 55718
(218) 384-4513
www.greenpasturesdairy.com

Kombucha
P.O. Box 19037
Encino, Ca 91416
www.kombucha2000.com

Kushi Store
Medicinal Quality Natural Foods
P.O. Box 500
Becket, MA, 01223
(800) 645-8744
www.kushistore.com

Main Coast Sea Vegetables
3 George's Pond Rd.
Franklin, ME 04634
(207) 565-2907
www.seaveg.com

Natural Import Company
Medicinal Quality Japanese Natural Foods
P.O. Box 2552
Asheville, NC 28802
(800) 324-1878
www.naturalimport.com

Really Raw Honey
3500 Boston St.
Baltimore, MD, 211224
(800) 732-5729
www.ReallyRawHoney.com

South River Miso
888 Sheldron
Conway, MA 01341
(413) 369-4057
www.southrivermiso.com

Powerkraut
Fresh organic and biodynamic
sauerkrauts and Kim Chi
S 7304 Gardner Road
Viroqua, WI 54665
organicpowerkraut@yahoo.com

SELECTED ORGANIZATIONS

Angelic Organics Learning Center
Classes and Courses
1547 Rockton Road,
Caledonia, IL 61011
www.learngrowconnect.org

Amberwaves
Journal of Planetary Health, Peace
and Organic Living
P.O. Box 487
Becket, MA 01223
(413) 623-0012
www.amberwaves.org

Dr. Hauschka Skin Care
20 Industrial Drive East,
South Deerfield MA, 01373
www.drhauschka.com

Josephine Porter Institute for
Applied Biodynamics
P.O. Box 133
Woolvine, VA 24185
(276) 940-2463
www.jpibiodynamics.org

Kolisko Institute
Research and Education in
Biodynamic Agriculture
PO Box 471
Santa Rosa, CA 95402
(707) 495-6604
www.kolisko.org

Kushi Foundation
Macrobiotic Research and Education
P.O. Box 390
Becket, MA 01223
(800) 975-8744
www.macrobiotics.com

LifeWays
Early Childhood Training
lifewaysnorthamerica@gmail.com

Lilipoh Magazine
P.O. Box 629
28 Gay Street
Phoenixville, PA 19460
(610) 917-0792
www.lilipoh.com

Michael Fields Agricultural Institute
Research and Training in Organic and
Biodynamic Agriculture
W2493 County Rd. ES
East Troy, WI 53120
(262) 642-3303
www.michaelfieldsarginst.org

North Central Region Biodynamic Group
Publications and Biodynamic Preparations
PO Box 2561
La Crosse, WI 54602
(608) 793-1193

The Pfeiffer Center Biodynamics
Chestnut Ridge, NY 10977
(845) 352-5020
www.pfeiffercenter.org

Rudolf Steiner College
Waldorf Teacher Training
Fair Oaks, CA
www.steinercollege.edu
(916) 961-8727

Rudolf Steiner Institute
*Courses in Spirituality, Art and
Social Change*
Green Mountain College, VT
www.steinerinstitute.org
(800) 774-5191

The Rudolf Steiner Library
65 Fern Hill Rd.
Ghent, NY 12075
(518) 672-7690
www.resteinerlibrary@taconic.net
Online library: www.waldorflibrary.org

The School of Spiritual Psychology
Classes, Seminars and Books
P.O. Box 7
Benson, NC 27504
www.spiritualschool.org

Sophia's Hearth Family Center
Guidance and Training
Keene, NH
www.sophiashearth.org
(603) 357-3755

Stella Natura
Biodynamic Calendars
P.O. Box 29135
San Francisco, CA 94129
(888) 516-7797
www.comphillkimberton.org

Sunbridge College
Waldorf Teacher Training
285 Hungry Hollow Road
Spring Valley, NY 10977
(845) 425-0055
www.sunbridge.edu

True Botanica
Supplements, Remedies, Cosmetics
Delafield, WI 53018
www.truebotanica.com
(800) 315-8783

Susun Weed
Wise Woman Center
P.O. Box 64
Woodstock, NY 12498
(845) 246-8081
www.susunweed.com

Waldorf in the Home
Resources for Nourishing Family Life
www.waldorfinthehome.com

Weston A. Price Foundation
Wise Traditions in Food, Farming
and Healing Arts
PMB 106-380
Wisconsin Avenue, NW
Washington, DC 20016
www.WestonAPrice.org

ANNE-MARIE FRYER WIBOLTT is a Waldorf class and kindergarten teacher, biodynamic farmer, author and natural health counselor. She has taught nutritional cooking and counseled for 25 years in her homeland Denmark, Europe and the United States. She trained as a macrobiotic cooking teacher and counselor and studied the principles of oriental medicine and the research of Dr. Weston A. Price before embracing the anthroposophical approach to nutrition, food and cooking. Anne-Marie co-authored with her husband a series of ten books on health and nutrition. She is currently working on another book, Cooking for and with Children, *Preparing for the Life of the Future.*

NATURAL HEALTH COUNSELING FOR LIFE

Natural and aesthetically well-balanced meals are the foundation for health, clarity of thought, equanimity in feelings, and the will to fulfill our life's purpose.

Anne-Marie Fryer Wiboltt offers sessions in person or by phone. For an introductory appointment, write Anne-Marie at info@cookingfortheloveoftheworld.com or phone her at (608) 648-2316.

The counseling sessions will help you create a living relationship with food and cooking. They will reawaken you to the beauty and polarities in nature and in your body, and stimulate a fresh and dynamic attitude to movement and exercise.

You will receive lasting support in creating a joyous life of health, inner peace, and happiness.

HEALING, AN INNER PATH

Healing involves deepening our connection to our spirit nature and the spiritual nature of the world. It is a process of restoring integrity to all areas and relationships in our lives, especially our relationship with food and cooking. Dis-eases in our soul or physical body guide us toward wholeness and present opportunities to rediscover our strength and trust in our inner knowing. The living art of cooking supports the healing processes. It is an enjoyable, health-giving, creative activity and an essential aspect of the healing path, the path of inner development.

COOKING FOR THE LOVE OF THE WORLD

Cooking classes and seminars, books and references, guidelines, articles, menus, and more. To learn more write to info@cookingfortheloveoftheworld.com or visit http://www.cookingfortheloveoftheworld.org

THE SCHOOL OF SPIRITUAL PSYCHOLOGY
A CENTER FOR CREATIVE SERVICE

THE SCHOOL OF SPIRITUAL PSYCHOLOGY is a center of learning and research designed to benefit society as a whole by fostering care for soul and spirit in individual life in conjunction with the renewal of culture as the meeting point between the human heart and the world. This enterprise focuses on more than technical training, intellectual comprehension, or individual inner development of a private nature. The programs and activities of the School serve the formation of capacities for consciously experiencing qualities of soul and spirit in oneself, in the profession and work one practices, in home life, community, and in the larger world. The School has operated since 1992 and serves people from all walks of life.

In 2004, the School moved to a new center in Benson, North Carolina, near Raleigh. The School operates a program in Sacred Service, a program in Spirit Healing, and Caritas: Caring for Those Who Have Died. The School's website is www.spiritualschool.org. The School also publishes a semiannual online journal that can be found at www.sophiajournal.org.